WELTS ON YOUR BUTT
A CALF COULD SUCK

by
Tom Brand

Richardson & Company Press

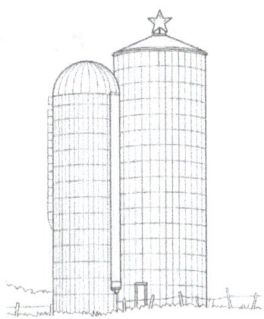

Welts on Your Butt a Calf Could Suck
Reflections on Faith, Family, and a Farm Kid's Life

Published by Richardson & Company Press
www.RichardsonPress.com

Cover, interior design, and illustrations by Tom and Beth Brand, with AI assistance under the creative direction of the author.

ISBN: 979-8-9987046-0-4
Library of Congress Control Number: 2025909423

For Beth—
who believed in me, even when I didn't.
This book exists because you never stopped
believing I had something worth saying.

TABLE OF CONTENTS

PREFACE

If you're reading this, I'll start by saying what every kid eventually learns to say when someone shows up:

Thanks for coming by.

These stories weren't written with a book in mind. They grew from columns written in the quiet margins of busy weeks—moments remembered during meetings, on Sunday afternoons, or long drives where the stories showed up like old friends. One memory would roll into another, and before I knew it, the words found their way to paper like they'd been waiting all along. Sometimes, they surfaced late at night—memories deeper than I expected. They started as columns under the title *That Hopkins Kid*, and to be honest, that still fits. Sure, I'm older now, but I'm still that kid—dirty boots, crooked smile, ink smudge on my hand, trying to make sense of the world by writing it down.

This book is a collection of memories, not a memoir. The difference matters: memoirs are polished; memories are dusted off, not scrubbed clean. What you'll find here are snapshots of small-town life—of farm chores and family gatherings, of well-meaning adults who shaped me, and friends who made sure I didn't take myself too seriously. It's equal parts heart and humor—with some column titles I never thought would see print, like *"Welts on Your Butt a Calf Could Suck."*

These pages are for anyone who grew up under wide skies and thought the local hardware store was magical. They're for those who remember what it meant for *Kool-Aid* to be done right—not that weak stuff someone mixed with too much ice and too little sugar. And they're for those who know freedom isn't just a word on a bumper sticker—it's something we live, and something others gave everything for.

Now—if you'll allow me one serious moment in a book that contains peacock sound effects and hog lot recollections—I need to say a few thank-yous.

To **Beth**, who has laughed with me, edited me, encouraged me, and never once rolled her eyes when I said, "I think this one might be worth writing down." You've shared every story, every memory, every mile, and every metaphorical Kool-Aid packet in this life. You listened to each of these as I read them aloud, sometimes as I shed tears of emotion, Thank you for loving the guy who still forgets what day the trash goes out. You're the steady hand in every paragraph.

To **Mom**—thank you for your faith. You've lived it daily, taught it quietly, and shared it freely. You taught me how to read, how to pray, and how to be patient... even when I tested all three of those lessons in the same day. Your gentle teaching, and deep belief in people (especially your children), has changed lives—whether you know it or not. You believed in creativity long before it was fashionable, and taught us that "bottom" was the polite word— though "butt" made for a better column. Your parents—Grandma and Grandpa Alexander—showed us what love looks like around a table full of food and a yard full of kids. Their legacy is still at work in us.

To **Dad**, who passed in 2020 but remains in every lesson I learned the hard way. He grew up tough—a kid from the other side of the tracks—and statistically, he probably wasn't supposed to turn out as strong and steady as he did. But he did—because a few key people believed in him, and because he decided their belief was worth living up to. And you always knew the job had to be done right. He believed in hard work, fair discipline, and that raising kids right was the best thing you could do with your time on Earth. He taught me how to work, how to stand my ground, and how to stand up for others. He also gave me one-liners that are still rattling around in my head—and probably in this book. I still hear his voice every time I pick up a tool—or a pen.

To **my kids**, thank you for making me a dad. It's the role I've loved the most. You've grown up in a different time, and in ways I never did, but you've made me laugh, think, and feel more than I ever expected.

To **Alex**, who we lost in 2015—you're in our hearts every single day. Your light, your humor, and your fierce love of life continue to echo in our home and in everything I do. I think about you in quiet moments and loud ones. You're always here.

Finally, to **you**—the reader. Maybe you grew up like I did. Maybe you didn't. But if any part of these stories makes you smile, or remember something (or someone) worth remembering, then I've done my job. You don't need to grow up in Hopkins to understand the joy of homemade ice cream, the sting of a glare during a flashlight-holding mishap, or the reverence that silence holds in a cemetery on Memorial Day.

As a kid, I listened to a lot of stories. I could have been off reading books, playing with toys, or chasing the dog through the backyard. But more often than not, I was sitting nearby, listening. I was surrounded by great storytellers—neighbors, farmers, relatives—people who didn't always know they were telling stories worth remembering. But I remembered. And now, I'm doing my best to pass them along.

These stories come with dust on the boots and a smile in the retelling. Some are about livestock, others about lemon drink, parades, or varmint hunts. But in all of them, there's a thread of gratitude—for family, for freedom, for faith, and for the way stories bring us home.

So grab a good chair, pour yourself a glass of real lemonade (no substitutes), and let the memories settle in.

Thanks again for coming by.

Tom

Brand

Tom Brand
Hopkins native. Lifelong listener.
Father, husband, grandpa, and grateful son.
Still collecting stories—and trying not to spill the good Kool-Aid on my shirt.

INTRODUCTION

In early 2024, I found myself in a strange but familiar place: at the end of something. I had just stepped away from a twelve-year run as the executive director of a national association—one tied to an industry I'd been part of my entire professional life. The decision was the right one, but it left me staring into the wide, open space of what came next. I didn't have a roadmap, but I did have this: it was winter, bitterly cold, and quiet enough for old memories to start making noise again.

One day, I posted a story on Facebook—just a simple reflection about a long-ago winter on the farm. I remembered doing chores with my dad and brothers, cleaning out the old farrowing house where twelve sows and their litters huddled against the cold. We spread straw bedding in that shed one Sunday morning when the air itself seemed frozen solid. I didn't think much of the story at the time. It had just been rattling around in my head, and it felt good to put it into words.

Kay Wilson, editor of the *Nodaway News Leader*, commented on the post and asked if she could run it as a guest column. I said yes. When she asked me to email it—so the formatting wouldn't get scrambled—I figured that would be the end of it. But it wasn't. After receiving it, Kay told me she'd welcome more. When I asked how often she might be interested, she mentioned she had just lost a regular contributor—and if I felt like sending something every week, that would be just fine.

So I said yes again.

I tossed around a few title ideas, but Kay suggested *That Hopkins Kid*. It was simple, true, and oddly fitting. I may have left Hopkins, but Hopkins hasn't quite left me.

Writing these columns opened doors to rooms in my mind I hadn't stepped into in years. I started remembering things—half-forgotten moments that came back to life as soon as I began writing them down. And not just the memories, but the joy of writing itself. After years of writing with deadlines, strategies, and goals in mind, I had nearly forgotten what it felt like to write for the sheer enjoyment of it—to sit down, revisit a moment, and let it unfold on the page.

This book is the result of that unexpected gift. It's a collection of those weekly columns—stories from small-town life, farm work, family chaos, and the kind of humor that tends to show up in everyday life.

Many of the pieces were tied to the season, a holiday, or whatever the weather was doing that week. Some have been updated, a few expanded, and others appear just as they originally ran in the paper. And a few... well, they may still be waiting for their turn in print.

Thank you for reading. I hope these stories bring back a few memories of your own.

FENCEPOSTS AND FIELDWORK

There's no better place to learn the difference between "close enough" and "do it right" than behind a feed bunk, hanging onto a panel while sorting livestock, or backing up a trailer with someone shouting directions you can't hear.

This section gathers stories from the early days—when the work was hard, the rules were simple, and the memories were made between chores, pranks, and quiet moments no one thought were important at the time.

Some of these stories come from fields and fencerows, others from gravel roads, farm kitchens, or riding shotgun in an old Jeep. But all of them taught something. About humor. About humility. About how to get through a long day without spilling your lemonade.

And yes—sometimes, about welts.

What we didn't know was that every moment was adding up to something bigger.

"Farming looks mighty easy when your plow is a pencil, and you're a thousand miles from the corn field."
— DWIGHT D. EISENHOWER

WELTS ON YOUR BUTT A CALF COULD SUCK

Working livestock brings out the best in people.

And by "best," I mean a full spectrum of emotions ranging from quiet prayer to loud, creative vocabulary—often in the span of minutes.

My dad, family, and I worked together in those moments—sorting hogs, moving cattle, building fence, hauling feed, fixing what broke, and re-breaking what was fixed. While Dad wasn't much for long speeches, he was a man of very specific instructions—and memorable delivery.

There was one line in particular that stuck with me when he wanted to make sure we understood consequences: "I'll put welts on your butt a calf could suck."

I didn't know what a welt was when I first heard it. But I did know about calves. I'd watched them go after their mothers like vacuum cleaners. If a welt was big enough to attract that kind of attention, I definitely didn't want one on my backside.

Dad did believe in spankings. But he also believed in fairness. He made sure we knew: "*I never gave you one you didn't have coming.*" And he was right.

That phrase became part of our family folklore. We'd laugh about it in later years—me, married with kids of my own, telling him I was going to write a book someday and title it exactly that. He chuckled. He knew I wasn't joking.

The moment I remember best took place in a hog lot, with a pile of steel panels we'd just dragged in to sort pigs. Dad told me plainly: "Don't let the hogs get on that pile. And if you do…"

Simple enough. Except hogs are naturally drawn to forbidden zones. They're like toddlers in steel-toed shoes. And just as Dad turned his back, they made a beeline for the pile.

I froze. My brain short-circuited for a second. Then that phrase rang out in my head like a starter pistol: *"welts on your butt a calf could suck."*

Suddenly, I was moving with the precision of a Navy SEAL. I cut off the hogs, waved my arms, yelled like a banshee, and did not let them get on that pile. To this day, I credit my reflexes entirely to the motivating power of that sentence.

When I had kids of my own, I never used that line. Not once.

But not because I didn't think about it—constantly.

Usually while holding a flashlight and watching the beam drift toward space like a confused lighthouse.

Did I want to say it? Absolutely.

Did I need to say it? Maybe not.

But man, it was right there on the tip of my tongue.

I sometimes wonder if Dad heard it from his dad.

It feels like something passed down through generations of men trying to raise kids, build fences, and keep hogs where they belong. A phrase born out of dirt and sweat, meant to do two things: get your attention, and get the job done.

Dad's been gone since 2020. But that line? That line is still alive and well in our family.

It's part of the soundtrack of my childhood—funny, firm, and unforgettable.

And now that I've lived long enough to tell the story, I say it with nothing but love.

Because some life lessons don't come with a diagram.

They come with a fence panel, a pen of hogs, and a dad who teaches you that doing it right matters—even if it takes a colorful turn of phrase to make it stick.

NO PICTURE, JUST MEMORY

Cold winter days bring back memories of growing up on the farm south of Hopkins—of sledding parties through church and 4-H, Christmas caroling, FFA fruit sales (and deliveries), and the daily rhythm of chores that waited regardless of the weather.

Ours was a diversified family farm that included a farrow-to-finish hog operation. That included the "new farrowing house," built by Morton Buildings, with 35 crates and a grower unit over a manure pit. But my favorite was the "old farrowing house," a converted building with twelve pens. The rest of the sows were housed in two- and three-pen sheds scattered around the place. All told, we had room for 110 sows, rotated through the system year-round.

My dad always said the best way to keep boys out of trouble was a five-gallon bucket and a bunch of sows. Looking back, he wasn't wrong. I don't recall my brothers—Joe or Bill—or me ever getting into much mischief. Between scraping concrete slabs, letting out seventy-five sows twice a day, and hauling feed by bucket to those in the sheds, there wasn't much time for trouble.

The old farrowing house and the sheds were bedded with straw. Hogs are surprisingly clean animals—most would do their business outside when let out—but cleaning and re-bedding was still part of the routine. With the manure spreader hitched behind a Farmall tractor, we'd go at it with pitchforks and scoops, clearing out the pens before spreading fresh straw and turning the sows back in with their litters.

Looking back now, very few memories compete with how much I enjoyed those mornings. The old farrowing house was always my favorite. The lights were low, the L.B. White heater hummed at one end, and the smell of fresh straw mixed with the low, rhythmic grunting of a sow nursing her litter. I remember standing there with Dad and my brothers for just a few quiet moments, not saying much—just listening, and taking it in.

I can't recall any pictures we ever took of the hog operation, and none at all of the straw bedding or the sheds. But honestly, the memory is sharper than any photograph. Maybe that's better. Photos fade, get lost in drawers or digitized into nothing. But the smell of straw, the feel of a pitchfork handle in your hand, the sound of piglets nursing—that kind of memory stays with you.

> "Pigs remind us that happiness lies in the beauty of simple pleasures."
> — JILL SCOTT

ADVENTURE ON WHEELS

One decision often leads to another, sometimes in ways that don't seem connected until you take a step back. My brother Joe drove a Buick Skyhawk—a dependable car that served him well. But maybe, just maybe, that Skyhawk planted a subliminal idea in his head—the urge to own something less practical and more adventurous. That might explain why he eventually found himself the proud owner of the polar opposite of a Buick.

We didn't travel to St. Joseph often, so I remember the trip well—Dad, Bill, Joe, and I loaded up to check out a vehicle Joe had seen advertised in the Penny Press. There, sitting in the driveway of our destination, was the real prize and purpose of our mission: a deep green CJ-5 Jeep. It had oversized tires on hurricane rims, an almost-new canvas top, and a few creative modifications. The black front seats had been borrowed from a Trans Am. The back seat was long gone, leaving a small storage area. A mysterious button on the side of the steering column—probably from the JC Whitney catalog—served as the horn. The mismatched steering wheel and three-speed, four-wheel-drive setup made this Jeep more than just transportation. It was an adventure on wheels.

The price? Exactly what the owner still owed: $600.

After a quick test drive and a paperwork shuffle, Brother Joe was no longer just a Buick owner—he was the captain of a rolling safari (though future wildlife patrols mostly involved checking cows in the pasture). I remember being jealous as Bill hopped in for the ride back to the farm.

Dust swirling, tires roaring—you couldn't even hear the radio, but everyone loved driving that Jeep. When the weather was warm enough, we pulled off the canvas top and embraced the adventure. The Jeep earned its keep, serving not just as reliable transportation but also as a tool for fencing, chores, and checking water gaps and cattle.

The combination of a canvas top and unlockable doors wasn't ideal for a college parking lot, so Joe drove the Skyhawk to Mizzou. That left me to keep the cobs cleaned out of the carb and drive the Jeep to high school. Seniors could drive to football practice, so it became my mode of transportation. You'd be surprised how many football players can fit in a CJ-5 with only two front seats.

It was two and a half miles from our house to the top of School House Hill in Hopkins. No matter how long the Jeep sat idling in the machine shed, it still took hitting the road for the heater to kick in—*2.4 miles*, to be exact, before anything resembling warmth was felt.

Like all good adventures, this one eventually ended. Several years after Joe bought the Jeep, it found a new owner—someone eager to take on gravel roads, pasture runs, and all its quirks. By then, the Trans Am seats were more worn, the horn button was still an oddity, and the heater was still slow. That CJ-5 was never just a vehicle. It was freedom on four wheels.: built for adventure, best enjoyed with the top off, dust in the air, and the radio drowned out by the hum of the road.

ROOSTER CALIBRATION

The KFEQ radio offices were on the top floor of the Provident Bank building, just off Frederick Avenue in St. Joseph. With its glass exterior, the building offered outstanding views in three directions. The farm studio sat on the east side, featuring a large window that opened into the main control room to the north and a smaller window to the left, offering a glimpse into the news booth.

The control room operator engineered the entire broadcast—handling commercial breaks, music, and audio segments you provided for on-air playback. They also managed network programming, ensured smooth transitions, and kept track of the clock. That operator was the heartbeat of live radio.

Each weekday morning before the six o'clock news, I read the Savannah school lunch menus, then wrapped up the hour with the weather forecast and local information. From my vantage point, I could see the master control clock and would backtime leading into the news. I watched the sweeping second hand, knowing exactly how much time was needed for the current weather conditions and the required legal ID before the top of the hour.

That morning, I misread the clock by a full 60 seconds. Rob Horning was in master control and gave me the look— then motioned that I still had a minute to go and slid on his headphones, ready to jump in if things went sideways. No worries. I'd been broadcasting long enough to know how to fill time.

I read the previous day's range of temperatures, the record highs and lows, and the sunrise time for the day. I noticed sunrise was at exactly 7 o'clock and, without thinking, said: "It's a perfect morning to calibrate your rooster." Without missing a beat, Rob asked how exactly one would do that.

So, I did what any undercaffeinated farm broadcaster would do—I made up a complete technique on the spot. It required just three tools: a portable radio (tuned to KFEQ), a rafter square, and a compass.

The owner would position the rafter square on the ground, using the compass to determine true north for the short side, with the longer arm pointing east and a clear view of the horizon.

It is easiest to calibrate your rooster when sunrise falls at the top or bottom of the hour, as the station's audio cues help ensure the bird stays in sync. A properly calibrated rooster will crow precisely when the news begins.

For roosters running behind schedule, you can speed them up by plucking a tail feather from the left side. For early-crowing birds, you can slow them down by plucking a tail feather from the right side. For extreme cases, if your rooster still crows off-schedule, you may need to reset his internal clock by whispering tomorrow's forecast into his left ear. If a rooster is too far out of compliance, the solution is simple: rooster noodle soup.

Through the years, listeners have told me they remembered hearing about rooster calibration, but I never met anyone who actually attempted the feat. But I like to think master control appreciated the perfect timing. When I'm occasionally asked for rooster calibration advice today, I usually begin with one simple question: "Is your rooster left- or right-footed?"

TAIL
FEATHERS

FIVE, SIX...PICK UP ROCKS

"One, two, tie your shoe. Three, four, shut the door. Five, six...pick up rocks."

That was dad's version of the old nursery rhyme. No skipping ropes or hopscotch here—just the rhythm of rural childhood, where rhymes came with a lesson and usually a little work. Especially in spring.

The worst offender was a field near the highway—the good Stuckenholz bottom ground, except for the fact that it seemed to double as a rock breeding ground each spring. Every thaw brought another batch to the surface. And not just little pebbles, either—rocks, chunks of broken concrete, and remnants from an old portable concrete plant buried long before I came along. It was like the earth itself didn't want to forget.

"Five, six, pick up rocks. Seven, eight...pick up more rocks." Dad would say it with a grin, proud of his original spin on a childhood jingle. He was serious about the work, but he wasn't above having a little fun at our expense. There were plenty of days I wondered who was enjoying the experience more—me, trudging through the disked field, or Dad, chuckling to himself as we picked up what the ground had so generously offered.

And yet, like most things with Dad, it stuck. Not just the rocks in the field, but the memory of that grin. That half-serious, half-smirking tone he used when he handed out jobs in verse.

Decades later, I caught myself using the very same rhyme—except with a slight edit. "Five, six, pick up sticks. Seven, eight, pick up more sticks." That was my version when it came time to clean up the backyard after a long winter and a squirrel-ravaged Chinese elm tree. My kids didn't love it any more than I had. They groaned, rolled their eyes, and dragged the sticks into a pile. They got the job done—which, of course, was Dad's goal all along.

19

There's a fencerow still out by that field. And if you know where to look, you'll still see a few of those bigger rocks and concrete chunks we hauled out all those years ago. They're silent now, safe from ever being scarred by the planter again. But to me, they're echoes of Dad's laugh—and that rhyme I thought I'd never repeat.

Funny how the lines we roll our eyes at as kids become the ones we pass along. Just with a different backyard, a different audience, and the same blend of humor and work ethic.

Because sometimes, the best traditions aren't found in family heirlooms or holiday recipes. They're found in a field, halfway through a made-up rhyme, with a pile of rocks and Dad smiling.

> "What one loves in childhood stays in the heart forever."
> — MARY JO PUTNEY

20

BELOW RADAR, ABOVE THE FIELD

The hum of a self-propelled windrower has a way of lulling you into a rhythm. The heat of the engine at your back, the steady rumble beneath you, the rotating header chewing through hay up front, the afternoon sun warming your shoulders—it all blends together into a sort of trance. Your stomach's still full from lunch, your eyes a little heavy, and the only thing you're worried about is keeping the row straight.

And then—a jet flies over.

Not just any jet. A screaming, afterburner-rattling blur, faster than your brain can process. It slices overhead, hugging the ground so tight you see it before you hear it. And by the time your heart has finished leaping into your throat, the sound finally hits—ripping through the sky like someone's tearing open the clouds.

That was part of life growing up on the farm just south of Hopkins. We were about 100 nautical miles from Offutt Air Force Base in Omaha—home to Strategic Air Command (SAC) during the Cold War. Those pilots trained to fly low—"bustin' radar," we called it—staying beneath the detection range of enemy systems. And apparently, our farm made for a pretty good checkpoint.

Our house, machine shed, barns, and other buildings sat above the 102 River bottom, with a pair of towering concrete silos that stood like sentinels. Whether they meant to or not, those pilots passed by often—maybe because of the silos, maybe because of the view, maybe just because they could.

We knew the stakes. SAC wasn't playing games. Between the missile silos scattered across Missouri and Whiteman Air Force Base in Knob Noster, we understood we were living on a Cold War chessboard—even in rural Nodaway County.

But the flyovers had their own charm. I lost count of the times I was mowing hay, miles from the house, and had the wits scared clean out of me by a jet buzzing overhead. I never got used to it. And honestly, I'm not sure I wanted to.

One time, I was feeding hogs out on the concrete slabs just south of the house and spotted the jet coming from the north. I climbed up on a hog panel, yanked off my red cap, and waved. I had no idea if they saw me—but they were so low I could see the pilot through the cockpit window. If they'd been flying any slower, I swear I could've read the name printed below the canopy.

A few minutes later, the pilot circled back. And this time, he was directly overhead, wagging his wings as he passed. That little tilt—that silent, yes-we-saw-you—was one of the biggest thrills of my young life.

They're gone now. SAC moved to Andrews Air Force Base in Maryland. The Cold War is over, and low-flying, radar-busting surprise visits are a thing of the past. There's no jet thunder. No wig-wags. No roar of engines just above the treetops.

The silos still stand, but the skies are quieter. Every now and then, when I'm in a field and I hear something high overhead, I still look up. And for a split second, I half expect to see a flash of silver cutting across the sky. Maybe even a wave from a cockpit window.

And I think about how, for a brief moment in the middle of a Cold War, in the middle of a field, two worlds met—one busting radar, one cutting hay.

And both smiled.

> "When once you have tasted flight, you will forever walk the earth with your eyes turned skyward."
> — RICHARD BACH

GOING TO THE SALE BARN

The trucks and trailers in the parking lot were like a variegated afghan of colors. Behind them, in penned lots, the color palette narrowed to variations of black, roan, and cream. Many of the dark-colored bodies had white faces, and a few still wore horns. The sights were matched by the distinct odors in the air—a blend of mud, livestock, and cook shack grease that clung to your coat long after you'd gone home. For a farm kid, going to the sale barn for a cattle sale wasn't an errand. It was a day out.

As a youngster, the newest location in our area was Merrigan Brothers Livestock Auction, northwest of Maryville. I remember stepping into the sale arena when the paint was still fresh and the risers looked clean enough to pass for bleachers. My brother and I would kill time on the catwalk that passed above the pens, watching the cowboys ride horseback as they sorted cattle for size and sorted them into groups for the ring. The air was thick with dust and noise, alive with hooves and hollers echoing off the rafters

Back in the arena, we'd find a spot near the top row and watch the action—cattle trotting in, the auctioneer's chant rolling like a drumbeat, the bidders below nodding or flicking a finger. I didn't understand much of it, but I knew better than to move around too much. I'd been warned: wave your hand at the wrong time and you might end up owning a steer. So I sat on my hands. Literally.

Cigarette smoke hung in the air—picking a seat with clean air was a strategy all its own. More than once, I fell asleep with my head against Mom or Dad, the auctioneer's rhythmic voice tugging me down into a warm, dusty nap.

There were several livestock markets within thirty or forty minutes of Hopkins. If we headed north, the sale barn in Bedford meant familiar faces. What I remember most there were the hay sales—bales auctioned in the parking lot like tailgate treasure before the livestock even started selling.

If we went east, we were headed for George Young's sale barn in Grant City. I always knew we were getting close when we passed the bank at Sheridan, then wound through the tree-lined stretch near Isadora that always looked like it belonged on a postcard.

To the northwest, the Crawfords ran the barn in Clarinda—another familiar stop. Each of these barns had a café, either tucked just inside the door or around the corner. And while the menus changed from town to town, two things were always worth betting on: pot roast with mashed potatoes, and homemade pie that reminded you someone's grandma was still working the kitchen.

Some of those barns are gone now. Others are still going strong, still hosting the quiet ritual of farm families gathering to buy, sell, visit, and swap stories between cups of coffee and the next lot to come into the sales ring. I haven't sat on a sale barn riser in a while, but every now and then, when the wind smells like hay and diesel and lunch, I remember how those days felt. They weren't just errands.

They were the kind of days that reminded you where you belonged.

"A community is the mental and spiritual condition
of knowing that the place is shared,
and that the people who share the place
define and limit the possibilities
of each other's lives."

— WENDELL BERRY

LEARNING TO SWIM

My dad was a storyteller. And among my favorites were the tales involving the Cross boys.

The one that always stuck with me was about the time they decided it was finally time for Haroldie to learn how to swim.

Dad said the brothers showed up at the 102 River, just north of Hopkins. Dean Cross made the announcement like it was a royal decree:

"Today's the day Haroldie learns to swim."

Then they grabbed Harold—who Dad guessed was maybe four or five years old—and chucked him straight into the water.

He sank like a rock.

A moment passed. Then another. Everyone watching started to worry. But sure enough, Harold surfaced, kicked his legs, moved his arms, and paddled his way to shore. Just like Dean said he would.

Not exactly a Red Cross certified technique—but apparently, it worked.

In a world full of statistics, one that stuck out to me was that 29% of Americans say they're afraid—or very afraid—of speaking in public. Another survey found that about a third are afraid to put their head underwater. Half are scared of the deep end.

Fortunately, I made peace with all three.

Like Harold Cross, I was probably four or five when I learned to swim—but my method was a little gentler.

Hopkins teacher Beccy Baldwin had a swimming pool in her backyard and taught lessons. Mom says I was hesitant at first, especially about putting my face in the water. But I remember how Beccy had me start by blowing bubbles—nothing fancy, just learning to trust the water.

Before long, I was paddling around with the confidence of a kid who hadn't been thrown in by his siblings.

Later on, I graduated to swimming lessons at the Bedford public pool. Red Cross certified, run by Pat Snyder and her daughters. Each summer, you picked up where you left off—basic, intermediate, advanced. I never got the official "lifesaver" badge, but I was confident in the water, and still am. That's something I'm grateful for even now.

———————————————————

Years later, we moved to St. Joseph. The house we bought came with a swimming pool—and a backstory.

The previous owner, Suzy Nothhouse, had taught swim lessons in that pool for forty years. She once told us, proudly and without exaggeration, "I taught half of St. Joe how to swim."

Turns out she wasn't kidding. As we met new people and told them where we lived, we kept hearing the same thing:

"Oh, I learned to swim there!"

There was one detail about Suzy's teaching style that stood out. If a kid didn't want to get in the water? She'd throw them in.

She said they usually figured it out.

Honestly, I've wondered if Suzy and Dean Cross might've been long-lost siblings.

> "Swimming is a confusing sport,
> because sometimes you do it for fun,
> and other times you do it not to die.
> And when I"m swimming,
> sometimes I'm not sure which one it is."
> — DEMETRI MARTIN

LAUGHTER AS A LIFE TOOL

Laughter is, without a doubt, one of the best medicines—especially when it comes at the expense of a well-executed prank. There's an art to it: where mischief meets mastery. The best practical jokes require patience, attention to detail, a tight lid on secrecy, and—if you're lucky—one or two co-conspirators who can keep a straight face. Add the element of surprise, and you're in business. Most people admire a good prank… especially if they're not the one cleaning up after it.

One of the earliest pranks I ever joined was the tradition of the chivaree—a good-natured ambush to welcome newlyweds home. Our group of friends and neighbors would arrive quietly, arm ourselves with pots and cowbells, then raise Cain until the newlyweds came to the door and invited us inside for sweets. I could barely contain my excitement, but it was worth it for the reward. I still remember the sound of the cowbells and the taste of a Snickers bar handed through the doorway.

My Aunt Helen Abbey was especially fond of mischief—and particularly enjoyed trying to pull one over on my dad. After a day visiting apple orchards, she quietly stashed a gallon jug of apple cider vinegar on the bottom shelf of the fridge. When Dad got home, she sweetly told him there was something cold waiting for him. I can still see her clapping with delight as he grabbed the jug by the handle, took a generous swig straight from the bottle—and immediately spat the whole mouthful into the sink, gagging and groaning. Aunt Helen's giggle was proof enough it had gone exactly to plan.

Dad himself had a hand in a few classics. Our neighbor, Danny Cline, had an unshakable loyalty to red equipment—specifically International Harvester. One day, after a repair project, Dad and my brother Bill painted the patched area bright John Deere green. I wasn't in on that one, but I took every opportunity to remind Danny of it… often.

College brought new opportunities for more elaborate pranks.

One of my favorites involved a friend—Travis Tamerius, king of practical jokes—and his beloved Ford Mustang.

I recruited a roommate to borrow his keys. Popped the hood. Rerouted a wire from the horn to the windshield wipers.

When he finally took it to the carwash, I made sure I was riding shotgun.

On the way home, he clicked the wipers—and with every swipe, the horn blasted the car in front of us.
The look on his face was pure satisfaction.

I'd perfected that trick years earlier by wiring the horn to the turn signals.

Sure, America's Funniest Videos and social media are full of stunts and silly moments—but the best kind of humor is homemade. The kind that grows from a shared grin, a little effort, and a perfectly timed surprise.

Life's too short to go through it without laughter. And if you can turn an ordinary Tuesday into a legendary story, well… that's time well spent.

"Humor can help you cope with the unbearable so that you can stay on the bright side of things until the bright side actually comes along"

— ALLEN KLEIN

YOU'RE A GOOD BACKER-UPPER

Some people are natural-born surgeons. Some are brilliant mathematicians. My dad? He was a gifted trailer-backer.

This is not a skill to take lightly. Backing a trailer is a specialized form of magic—an ancient rite performed with a steady hand, a sharp eye, and the patience of a saint.

I, unfortunately, did not inherit this talent.

My children can confirm.

Every August, our family made the pilgrimage to the Missouri State Fair. For over a decade, I broadcasted live from Sedalia during the fair's eleven-day run. Some years, we borrowed or rented a camper and camped on the fairgrounds—cramming our version of "family vacation" into the heat, dust, and deep-fried chaos of the State Fair.

One year, we brought the rented camper home early to pack before heading out. My job? Back it into the driveway.

That's where things fell apart.

The driveway had a slope. The trailer had a mind of its own. And my backing skills were… let's call them *aspirational*.

Beth, in the role of spotter, did her best. It took multiple attempts. I got frustrated. Then more frustrated. And like all great marital stress tests, this one happened in full view of our kids—particularly our oldest, Morgan, who was six at the time and soaking up every moment like a little sponge in sparkly shoes.

Eventually, we got the camper in place, packed up, and headed to what I lovingly called our "11 days in purgatory." Life moved on.

Morgan, as we soon discovered, did not forget a thing.

Months later, we inherited a backyard playhouse from my niece and nephew. It was the perfect size for our kids. My dad loaded it onto a trailer and made the 50-mile haul to deliver it. We took down a section of chain-link fence so he could back it into place.

Then Dad went to work.

From the street, into the ditch, across the lawn, curving around the house, weaving past the Chinese Elm all the way to the back yard—it was like watching choreography. One fluid motion. No hesitation. Not a word needed. He set the brake and hopped out like it was nothing.

And that's when Morgan, watching with the seriousness only a six-year-old can muster, delivered the verdict. It's a line that will live forever in family lore:

"Momma, you should have married Grandpa. He's a good backer-upper."

Ouch.

It was one of those moments where you want to laugh, cry, and immediately enroll in trailer-backing school.

That little playhouse still sits in our backyard. We recently cleaned it out for the next generation to enjoy. The two oldest grandsons, Micah and Shiloh, helped—hauling out old toys, brushing away cobwebs. They haven't had much time to make memories in it yet, but I can already picture the tea parties, Nerf battles, and popsicle breaks ahead.

And when they do finally make it their own, I'll be standing there grinning—because that playhouse will always be the site of one of the most honest critiques I've ever received.

Somewhere up there, I'm sure Dad is smiling. Probably backing an angel's hayrack into a tight corner, just to show off.

> "A good backer knows where they've been,
> where they're headed,
> and how to make it all look effortless."
> — ANONYMOUS

FAITH, FAMILY, AND FRONT YARDS

Every family has its own soundtrack. Ours played in a key of peacocks calling across the field, the sizzle of a grill, and laughter drifting through screen doors. In this section, the scenes shift to parades and potlucks, holiday memories, and Sunday mornings that lingered in your heart long after the hymnals were closed and the ice cream had melted. These aren't just traditions—they're the shorthand for love, belonging, and a well-worn Tupperware container carried home with pride.

"Rejoice with your family
in the beautiful land of life."
– ALBERT EINSTEIN

SUNRISE IN THE CEMETERY

Growing up on the farm, getting up before sunrise was part of the rhythm. Chores don't wait for the sun, and neither did Dad. Whether we were headed to let out hogs to feed, build fence, or get a jump ahead of the weather, I was familiar with what the day looked like before the first light peeked over the eastern horizon.

But one spring morning carved its place in memory. It wasn't about hogs, building fence, or chores. We were headed to the cemetery.

One Easter Sunday, just as the sky began to lighten, we trekked north of Hopkins and gathered with other members of the church at the cemetery for a sunrise service. Even as a kid, rubbing sleep from my eyes and trying to button a jacket with cold fingers, I knew something about the moment was different. It was a different kind of quiet, a stillness.

In that silence, we reflected on the women who, 2,000 years earlier, rose early to make their own walk to a cemetery. They didn't bring lawn chairs or hymnals; they brought spices and grief. They came to anoint the body of Jesus, only to find the stone rolled away and the tomb empty. The range of emotions was endless. Shock. Fear. And then—the angel's words: "Do not be afraid. He is not here. He is risen."

That's what we came to remember. That's why we stood there among the headstones. We weren't mourning; we were celebrating. And as the sun crested over the hill, someone would begin a hymn without any instrument but the ones God gave us.

"Low in the grave He lay, Jesus my Savior." And then, it would come. Every voice singing: "Up from the grave He arose! With a mighty triumph o'er His foes."

There's something about singing that particular song as the sunlight stretches across a cemetery that gives you a chill deeper than the morning breeze of spring. Surrounded by reminders of mortality, there was a declaration of victory over death. Right there on ground that normally hosts somber occasions, we sang about the most joyful reversal in history.

We'd sing *"He Lives!"*, too—another favorite. Even now, I can hear voices around me, warm from years of use, their voices echoing the final line: "You ask me how I know He lives? He lives within my heart."

When I was younger, I think I sang that line mostly from memory. These days, I sing it from experience.

The names on the stones around me have become more familiar with time—some of them family, some of them friends, all of them part of the story. And yet, each Easter sunrise reminds me that the story isn't over.

That early morning in Jerusalem didn't just change history—it changed eternity.

Because no matter how cold the morning, or how heavy the past year may have been, Easter reminds us that light always breaks through. That the tomb is still empty. And that hope is still alive.

"He lives, He lives, Christ Jesus lives today. He walks with me and talks with me along life's narrow way."

And sometimes, He meets you at the cemetery—just as the sun comes up.

> "Our Lord has written the promise of resurrection,
> not in books alone,
> but in every leaf in springtime."
> — MARTIN LUTHER

MAY DAY

Tucked between the last frost and the first mowing of the season is one of the most overlooked holidays on the calendar: May Day.

Not many people make a fuss over it these days, but when I was a kid, May Day meant baskets, mischief, and a dash of sugar-fueled espionage. What I thought was a simple little tradition involving cookies, cut flowers, and the occasional banana bread slice turned out to have a history longer than I imagined.

Some quick research revealed that May Day has been around for over 2,000 years. Its most iconic symbol—the maypole—is a tall wooden pole decorated with ribbons and flowers, around which people would dance in celebration of spring. While I personally never risked ribbon entanglement, I've seen plenty of cheerful photos of kids giving it a go. In places like Minneapolis, they still do. Hawaii celebrates the day as Lei Day. Italians call it the happiest day of the year. Some even say it's the last chance fairies have to visit Earth before their seasonal visa expires. (I'm not sure when the window opens back up for them to visit again, but then, I've never seen a fairy.)

For me, May Day was about the baskets. Homemade, humble, and packed with treats: cookies, candies, banana bread, and cut flowers from the yard. We'd line those little green strawberry containers with wax paper, dress them up a bit, and head out on our mission.

The key was stealth. Drop the basket on the porch, knock or ring the bell, and run like you just committed a misdemeanor. Legend had it that if you were caught, you owed the recipient a kiss—which, for a kid, was reason enough to train for this like it was a track event. One would sneak up to the front door and place the basket where it could easily be found. A quick retreat back to the car was necessary to avoid getting caught. From there, we'd wait to see the response. If no one answered, we'd try again—knock, ring, and run back even faster.

We left baskets for Grandma, who always "just happened" to miss us and called later with a voice full of delight. Other deliveries went to folks in town—Doris Allen, Opal Orme, and several others—each one a successful mission, no kisses incurred.

Looking back, it wasn't about the banana bread or the wax paper. It was about doing something simple and kind, just for the joy of it. There aren't a lot of holidays built around anonymous generosity anymore. But I think about May Day every spring. Not just for the flowers or the folklore, but for those small, sneaky acts of kindness—and the people who made them feel magical.

May your basket, wherever it is, overflow with laughter, gifts from a loved one, and perhaps a sprinkle of fairy magic.

> "The best kind of mischief is the kind that comes with cookies, flowers, and a clean getaway."
> — ANONYMOUS

The tradition carries on through our oldest daughter, Morgan, and her kids. She's shared how they fill homemade baskets with candy, baked goods, and flowers from their yard, sneaking them onto neighbors' porches with the same kind of giggles. Micah and Shiloh take the lead on the dash-and-drop, while Eden, in a bright dress stitched by BeBe, twirls nearby like a tiny spring fairy. Even across the years and miles, the simple magic of May Day still finds a way to bloom.

VOICES I STILL HEAR

Some of my earliest memories stretch back to the days when my age could be counted on one hand. Many of those memories are connected to going to church and singing. I loved to sing and within a short amount of time, I had many favorites and knew where they could be found in the hymnal. *In the Garden* was found on page 99 and *Amazing Grace* was just a few turns away on page 140. Page 260 was my absolute favorite, *Standing on the Promises*.

I found as I grew older, the hymnal was just something to have in your hand in case you forgot the words. Once I started singing parts, the hymnal was essential, as it served as reference for the notes to sing. I was thankful to know the words so I could follow the notes instead of splitting my attention between the words and notes. With time, even the harmonies on the "standards" were easy to remember, too. It was remembering verses three and four that kept the hymnal in hand.

My oldest brother, Bill, was (and still is) an excellent piano and organ player. It's one thing to be able to play the notes on the page in the rhythm they were written. But what makes Bill excellent on the keys is his ability to hear the song and know there are parts that need to be played a little slower, faster, softer or louder. It doesn't matter if he is playing the piano or organ, he has a special ability to feel the song and the response from the congregation. The vision of him reaching down to open up the pipes on the organ is seared into my memory; I knew when I saw that how much more alive the music was going to become!

There's a full section of hymn and song lyrics with their own library among the rooms of my mind. Those are enriched as I remember Mom singing alto, Dad singing lead, and Bill playing. Paired with their friends, Wayne and Martha White, their sound was wonderful as Wayne added bass and Martha added her beautiful voice on lead, too. Memories like these make it a wonderful place to visit.

What Easter Sunday would be complete if we didn't sing #386? It's one of those hymns that as soon as the organ plays the introduction, you know the song within a few notes. Everyone loves the chorus, but the notes of the first verse, hearing the men's voices sing, and telling the story are necessary ahead of the chorus. *"Low in the grave He lay, Jesus my Savior! Waiting the coming day, Jesus my Lord!"*

Then, the chorus: *"Up from the grave He arose! Like a mighty triumph o'er his foes. He arose a victor of the dark domain, and He lives forever with His saints to reign. He arose! He arose! Hallelujah! Christ arose!"*

Even now, when we visit other churches, I still flip through the hymnal, curious to see where the old favorites fall—just to check if "Standing on the Promises," "In the Garden," or #386 are still holding their place.

These days, contemporary music takes up more space in the service. But every now and then, one of the old hymns makes its way in—and when it does, the room changes. The voices grow louder. Familiar smiles appear. People who hadn't sung a word suddenly join in—not always on pitch, but always from the heart.

Because those hymns still have a home in us.

And when we sing them, it feels a little like coming home.

POPCORN, ICE CREAM, AND RED BRICKS

Grandma and Grandpa Alexander's place—just two-thirds of a mile through the field and pasture, or a four-minute drive on country roads—was the backdrop for my Sunday afternoons and evenings.

In the days before cable or satellite TV, we considered ourselves lucky to get four channels: ABC from St. Joseph, and NBC, CBS, and PBS from Omaha. With the antenna angled just right, CBS would come in clear enough for *The Lawrence Welk Show*, *Hee Haw*, and *60 Minutes*, setting the scene for the routine that made those evenings priceless.

After my thorough review of the Sunday funnies from the *Des Moines Register* and *St. Joseph News-Press*, I'd head to the bedroom where the red plastic bricks in their cardboard tube were stored in the closet. Sometimes, there would be an unfinished architectural creation waiting on a contact paper-covered board under the bed. Complete with white windows and garage doors that actually opened, those blocks weren't just toys—they were tiny invitations to imagine, build, and create something new every time.

Supper typically consisted of popcorn and apples. Grandma had a variety of ways to fix popcorn—from the skillet or pot to a stovetop "whirley" popper with a crank handle. She eventually upgraded to a West Bend popper whose cover doubled as a bowl. The new one was easier. But somehow, the popcorn from the skillet always tasted just a little better.

As the evening wore on, Grandma would ask who wanted ice cream.

Dad would ask what kinds she had. If she said 'vanilla and Neapolitan,' he'd grin and ask, 'Got any chocolate chip?' She didn't. So he'd settle for vanilla. The next week, she'd have chocolate chip. Then he'd ask for Rocky Road.

And on it went. Week after week.

As a kid, I wondered how she never caught on. Now, I think she just liked playing along. It was their little game. Their rhythm.

The time together always passed quickly. Shortly after the Sunday Night Movie ended, the red brick creation was either disassembled or slid back under the bed for next time. The sorbet cups went into the dishwasher, and we'd head toward the car. Grandma and Grandpa would follow us out, and we'd wave goodbye as we made the short drive home.

We often take for granted the simple gift of proximity — the ease of a short drive, the time spent with people who love you. I'm thankful for those Sunday nights. For the popcorn. For the ice cream. For the bricks under the bed and the waves goodbye.

They were ordinary evenings. And they turned into lifelong memories.

> "Sometimes
> you will never know
> the value of a moment
> until it becomes a memory."
> — DR. SEUSS

I wasn't looking for them, but there they were — hundreds of red Elgo American Plastic Bricks, just like the ones I used to build with at Grandma and Grandpa's house. I didn't hesitate. I bought the whole set, scrubbed them clean, and smiled like a kid finding buried treasure, already picturing the grandkids playing with them someday.

Two pieces of plywood with contact paper have been tucked away for future masterpieces. Maybe I'm too old to play with bricks now. Just to be sure, I built a small house. (Turns out, I've still got it.) Someday, I'll show the boys all the expert techniques I mastered during my glory days as a world-renowned builder — at least in Grandma's living room. Some things you never really leave behind — you just carry them forward.

A FEW GOOD DOGS

I never walked to the end of a gravel driveway alone.
Not really.

There was always a dog trotting just ahead, or just
behind, or already waiting there for me.

I'm uncertain who to attribute the quote I've heard
about dogs for most of my life: "Every man is entitled to
one good wife and two good dogs." There's no argument
I've been blessed with a good wife—Beth and I have been
married for over 30 years. My allotment of good dogs has
easily exceeded two.

We always had dogs on the farm—some better at their
jobs than others—but the truly great ones weren't just
helpers. They were family. And the best of them all was Daisy.

The original Daisy, I should say. Blonde, sharp-eyed,
part English and Australian Shepherd, she understood
livestock better than some people. She worked the chute
like an extra set of hands—offering a bark here, a nudge
there—knowing exactly where to stand and when to stand
still. But as skilled as she was in the lot or pasture, she was
just as at home playing tag in the yard with Joe and me. She
never tired of the game. And when the tangle of kid and
dog legs knocked one of us over, she'd act hurt just long
enough to make us come check on her—then stick her nose
right in your eye and sprint away, tail wagging, grin wide.

She gave us a litter of pups—just a stretch from the
house, in the doghouse. It was a farm kid's introduction to
the miracle and mess of new life. But nothing prepared me
for losing her.

She died while we were away on a family trip. I was
12. The vet said it was parvo—probably brought in by
birds. Several of my classmates lost dogs the same way that
summer. The drive home from Colorado was unusually
quiet. And I've never stopped wishing I could've said goodbye.

Years later, another Daisy came into our home—a Shih
Tzu this time, with a very different personality, but the

same way of crawling into our hearts and making herself at home. She was the perfect family dog. She slept at the foot of our bed—burrowed all the way under the covers in winter—and would bark right back at the neighbor dogs like she had something big to say.

She gave us three litters of pups. There was the Biblical batch: Shadrach, Meshach, Abednego, Faith, and Hope. Then came the floral litter: TP, Lily (who didn't make it), and Violet. And finally, the Seinfeld group: Jerry, George, Elaine, Kramer, and Newman. Each one of them came with stories, lessons, laughter—and a little heartbreak, too. But I wouldn't trade the experience for anything.

Then came Harper.

We hadn't meant to get her. We'd gone to pick out a pup for Dad for Father's Day, and instead left with two— one for him, one that came home with us. Harper quickly became Alex's dog. They were inseparable. He'd hide in closets, she'd find him. He'd race down the hallway, she'd chase with a tail blur of excitement. Alex even rigged up an old starter from a grill that gave her a little zap (which she loved, somehow), and she'd come back for more.

When Alex started working at Chick-fil-A, Harper waited by the door every night for him to come home.

And after he passed, she kept waiting—for weeks. Same spot. Same time.

That's the kind of loyalty you can't train. You just hope to witness it once in your life.

Gency Jo came along a few months later. Her name came from a hospital visit where our daughter Zoe saw the emergency room sign only partially lit—just "GENCY." We all agreed that sounded exactly like the name an English Bulldog would choose for herself.

She was supposed to be Zoe's dog, but when Zoe left for school, Gency became mine. My shadow. My grumpy little co-pilot. She's compact—just 42 pounds—but built like a cinder block with legs. The vet calls her "sporty petite," but I just call her a cover hog who sleeps between Beth and me and pushes hard against your side when she's cold. She snores, drools, passes gas, and takes her job of looking important very seriously.

I've always joked that if she could flap her ears hard enough, she might actually achieve liftoff.

So yes, the list goes on: Cagney the Shih Tzu, who learned party tricks between songs at the radio station. Pete the Jack Russell, who Dad swore was this close to speaking English. Rowe the golden doodle. Harper. Gency. Daisy and Daisy.

And every single one left a mark.

Dogs are funny like that.

You think you're just getting a pet.

But what you're really getting is a best friend, a teacher, a comedian, and a keeper of secrets.

They walk beside you during the best years of your life—and wait by the door during the worst.

So maybe every man is entitled to one good wife and two good dogs.

But I've been lucky.

I've had more than my share of both.

"The more I learn about people,
the more I like my dog."
— MARK TWAIN

THE HOPKINS PICNIC

The community of Hopkins was platted in 1870 and had matured into a bustling teenage town of nearly one thousand residents when the Hopkins Picnic was first held in 1888. Except for a pause during the World Wars and the COVID-19 pandemic, the Hopkins Picnic has been a steadfast tradition. Though the 64461 ZIP code is no longer where I receive my mail, attending annually remains a strong connection to my roots.

For those who've ventured into town on Highways 148 or 246, or maybe have come on State Route JJ in the past, you know we simply refer to the summer celebration as "the Picnic." The Picnic is a gathering of friends, neighbors, family, and guests visiting from all over. As a youngster, I remember the streets packed by the thousands as the population of our little town swelled for those three days each summer.

Evans United rolled in with trucks full of metal and magic, assembling rides that blinked to life along Barnard Street and spilled onto Third—just a block from the stage where voices and fiddles would carry late into the night. Merchants' windows were filled with clubs and organizations' window displays, the local 4-H club had an achievement day ahead of the county competition, and a variety of groups and high school classes offered refreshments, raffle tickets, or the chance to sink the next victim at the dunking booth. It was most common to see people carrying their lawn chairs to sit in as they enjoyed the free entertainment on the stage or as a place to rest when not dancing. Entertainment was selected to appeal to a diverse audience and included area bands, "good neighbor" night with talent from other communities, square dancing, a queen contest, kiddie pedal pull, and street dances to cap off the evening.

My grandma, Cuma Alexander, enjoyed the Ferris wheel and we made a tradition of riding it together no matter our ages. To this day, I'm convinced the Ferris wheel ran a little faster on Saturday nights; Grandma would usually delay our ride together until Saturday evening.

Whether you live in town or only make it back once in a while, the Picnic has a way of pulling you in. You'll see familiar faces—classmates, cousins, neighbors you haven't seen since last year—and maybe share the same conversations you always do. You'll wait in line for a sandwich at the food stand, listen to music drifting from the stage, and catch yourself smiling at the lights on the Ferris wheel. Time changes towns, but some traditions hold their ground. And for a few nights every summer, Hopkins felt like the biggest small town in Missouri.

"Living in a rural setting exposes you
to so many marvelous things—
the natural world and the particular texture
of small-town life."
— SUSAN ORLEAN

These days, the Hopkins Picnic isn't as crowded as it once was. The world spins faster now, and small-town traditions are easy to overlook. But still, every summer, the lights rise over the streets, the rides blink to life, and the air fills with the sweet, familiar scent of popcorn, funnel cakes, and smoke from the grill. Food stands are open for business again, and neighbors lean into conversations that pick up right where they left off. There's a little more elbow room these days—but maybe that only makes the laughter carry farther. For a celebration that first took root more than 150 years ago, that's no small thing. In a world so quick to forget, Hopkins still remembers.

TRAINING RACING PIGS

Heinold Hogs bought thousands of hogs from farmers in the area during their time in business on the northeast side of Maryville. At their peak, they boasted locations across nine states. While livestock producers knew them for their purchasing power, Heinold was also known for something a bit more unusual: their team of racing pigs, showcased at state fairs throughout the Midwest.

So in 1988, as the Hopkins Picnic prepared to celebrate its 100th anniversary, our FFA chapter got an idea.

As chapter president, I attended the planning meetings and brought up the idea of inviting the Heinold Pig Races to town. It felt like the perfect fit. But we learned the company was disbanding their racing team and wouldn't be able to attend.

That's when our advisor, Dick Baldwin, leaned in with the kind of suggestion that changes everything:

"Why don't we train our own?"

And so we did.

That spring, we selected 10 shoats weighing around 40 pounds from our farm as promising contenders. (Author's note: Does anyone call a young, weaned pig a shoat anymore? It has been some time since I heard someone use the word, so in the interest of keeping the word in circulation, I've used it here.) Each showed just enough spunk to suggest they might enjoy a new career path. A dirt lot south of our house became the training grounds. We laid out a 120-foot horseshoe track using hog panels. Mr. Baldwin built a five-slot starting gate with repurposed disc springs that would fling open with the pull of a lever. We used a telephone bell Bob Whipple helped us wire up at the starting gate at first, but after it met its end falling from the fence, we swapped in a cowbell. It had more... showmanship anyway.

Bob Greenlee of ADM Feeds and community supporter Maurice Peve chipped in with feed—and, more

47

importantly, a steady supply of Oreo cookies. One taste of those Oreos was all it took. The pigs quickly learned that victory tasted sweet—literally. Over the course of a few weeks, we decreased the number of cookies, eventually ending with just one. Pigs, which are intelligent, learned the victor got the lone sweet treat.

Twice a day, chapter members (often accompanied by Mr. Baldwin) came to the farm to run the pigs through their paces. At first, the pigs had to be herded around the track. But after enough laps—and enough cookies—they started taking their marks like pros, stretching out their legs at the gate, focused and twitchy with anticipation.

We gave them names: Frankenswine, Miss Piggy, Kermit the Hog, and others equally pun-worthy. My mom sewed colorful cloth belts with numbers on them, which we strapped around their bellies so the crowd could easily choose their favorite. Mr. Baldwin made me the track announcer. I'd call out the names, hype the crowd, and sell 50-cent "chances" on each pig. (Not betting. Terminology mattered.)

We added a second fence a few feet outside the track to prevent overzealous children from distracting the pigs—though in fairness, the pigs loved the attention. That buffer zone also gave our FFA members room to move through the crowd, selling chances and stoking the energy.

By the time the Picnic rolled around in July, we had clean pigs (bathed in a horse tank before making the trip to town), a starting gate, and a full evening lineup. We ran races on the hour, each one ending with a victorious pig gobbling the lone Oreo cookie, while the rest enjoyed a little feed in the pan. Those who didn't win watched the winning pig with what can only be described as **existential snack regret**.

To keep it interesting, we sometimes added hurdles—a pipe laid across the track—which most pigs cleared like it wasn't there. But every now and then, one would stumble, and the crowd would erupt with laughter.

Speaking of the crowd… they loved it.

Most races had hundreds packed into and around the tent. Kids cheered, grown-ups clapped, and I wouldn't be surprised if a few side bets were made. After each race, we did a second-chance drawing using the losing tickets— handing out toy tractors, hats, and other premiums. It was part entertainment, part education, and all energy.

We even took the show on the road—running one more set of races the next weekend at the Nodaway County Fair. Then, like any good farm animals, the pigs returned home, resumed normal pig duties, and were eventually finished out with the rest of their litter mates. I like to think their hams were a little sweeter and their loins a little leaner. Fame and plenty of workouts will do that to a hog.

But for one sweet, glorious summer, they were stars. And so were we.

A group of high school farm kids, an ag teacher with a vision, and ten motivated shoats turned a centennial picnic into something unforgettable.

All it took was teamwork, a cowbell, and a few hundred Oreos.

FLOATING THE 102 RIVER

Most folks call it the one-oh-two river, or just simply the one-oh-two. Those who farm or live near it know how powerful the river can be and the amount of water it carries, especially after a rain. With the 102 as a backdrop in life at the ballpark, forming the border of the bottom ground on our farm, and seeing it regularly, the idea of floating a stretch of the river on an innertube appealed to me. I'd dreamt of such an adventure for years and finally decided it was time to give it a try.

I enlisted my best friend, Kyle O'Riley, his girlfriend (now wife) Mendi, and my girlfriend (now wife) Beth for the adventure. We planned to start at the north end of the farm and float downstream to the 102 River bridge on the Rancho del Rayo bottom—a journey I estimated would take a couple of hours. In my mind, it was like a scene from a movie and an adventure we'd share with friends and future generations.

Beth was unable to join us, which should have been the first omen I recognized. Leaving a vehicle at the southern landing point took longer than expected. Once we started, it was just a few hundred yards downstream before we began to bottom out. Another bad sign. We carried the tubes for a few hundred yards before trying again. The water had very little movement, but we were determined to enjoy our scenic river cruise.

There was some success, but with daylight fading and having made it only about a third of the way, we knew it was best to abandon ship, crawl up the banks of the river, and cut across the field to the highway.

We emerged mid-field and trudged along the edge to the end rows, then began cutting across to the roadway that would take us south where our truck was parked. Carrying tractor tire innertubes proved to be more challenging than simply tucking one under your arm. Daylight was fading, and it became clear we wouldn't reach the truck before dark.

I'm uncertain if it was relief or fear when I spotted a familiar vehicle coming down the highway and turning into the field. Aware of our plan and the encroaching darkness, our rescuer had grown concerned and decided to come check on our delay. We were grateful to see him—but I knew it probably wouldn't be a jovial greeting.

The first thing he said was, "Of all the stunts you've ever pulled, this one puts the icing on the cake." It was my dad. He was right. My planning had holes in it, and I was smart enough to know it—no excuses, no arguing the facts.

As years have passed, we've told the story dozens of times, always with a smile. The icing on the cake doesn't taste so bad now—but at the time, it sure lacked the sweetness we'd dreamed of.

"Eventually, all things merge into one,
and a river runs through it.
The river was cut by the world's great flood
and runs over rocks from the basement of time.
On some of those rocks are timeless raindrops.
Under the rocks are the words,
and some of the words are theirs."

— NORMAN MACLEAN,
from *A RIVER RUNS THROUGH IT*

I WANTED TO BE AN ASTRONAUT

The space race was quickly fading in the minds of most Americans by the mid-1970s. Instead, we turned our eyes toward the heavens, knowing there were men orbiting the planet in a space station called *Skylab*. The collaboration between the U.S. and Soviet Union gave us the *Apollo-Soyuz* missions, and an astronaut from Longmont, Colorado, commanded the module on one of those flights. Our Aunt Helen, who lived in Longmont, sent a newspaper clipping of the astronaut to Dad, along with a note suggesting there might be a family resemblance. After all, Longmont's favorite son—Vance DeVoe Brand—shared the same last name.

At the same time, my great Aunt Marie in Houston regularly sent clippings about what was happening at NASA. Once she learned I was infatuated with the space program, she started bringing me trinkets and other space-themed items whenever she came to visit. Add in the rerun episodes of *Star Trek* on television, the dreams of adventure, and the allure of exploring the unknown, and it was the perfect mix for a young mind. I was going to be an astronaut.

The fascination with space continued for years. Brother Joe and I would camp out in the backyard in the summer, where we witnessed meteor showers, the northern lights, and observed constellations. I was seven years old when the first group of shuttle astronauts was introduced. There was renewed excitement among the public as the thought of building a craft that could be launched, returned to Earth, and reused again was getting closer to becoming a reality.

The launch of the first Space Shuttle came in April 1981. I set my alarm clock for the middle of the night, camped out in the living room, waiting through countless countdown delays. Finally, just minutes before it was time to head out the door to catch the school bus, the Space Shuttle *Columbia* lifted off the launchpad. Just a little over two days later, it returned.

Eventually, my dreams of space shifted to something else. But still today, the dreams of adventure and exploration instilled by those early influences have never left me. Perhaps that's why I still find myself looking up at the stars, imagining the possibility of an adventure to space.

What became of the astronaut from Longmont, Colorado? Vance Brand was involved in several missions; in addition to the Apollo-Soyuz mission, he was a commander for three shuttle missions on both *Columbia* and *Challenger*, with a career that spanned from 1966 to 1990, and he remained active with NASA until his retirement in 2008. After retiring from NASA, he made his home in rural California. While we've never found a direct connection in the family tree, I'll always claim the astronaut as a "cousin" who adventured in space.

Vance DeVoe Brand. The name feels familiar—and for a kid dreaming of space, that was more than enough.
Photo courtesy of NASA

A SECOND FAMILY, WELL DONE

It took eighteen years to meet family members I never knew existed. This newfound family didn't originate from the Brand or Alexander family tree. In fact, if you were to do an Ancestry.com DNA test, I doubt we'd share much genetic connection. However, we both have European roots—mine in the west, theirs in southeastern Europe.

It was the fall of my first year at Mizzou when one of the guys in the house where I lived invited me to join him for supper at a family-owned steakhouse in Columbia. When I heard the word "steakhouse," I was hesitant—I was trying to stick to a budget. But after hearing how their house special was affordable and everything on the menu was great, I was convinced. Within a few minutes, I found myself in a steakhouse in a strip mall just off I-70 and Stadium Boulevard.

Stepping into that steakhouse, we were greeted by guys cooking at the grill just inside the door. Picking up a tray, we gathered our silverware and began to work our way down the line—grabbing a salad, adding dressing, and picking out a dessert. I ordered "the special," an eight-ounce sirloin with a choice of fries or baked potato, a salad, a slice of Texas toast, and a drink. The price? Just $4.95.

The atmosphere of this steakhouse is classic—a configuration of booths around the perimeter with tables in the center of the dining room. A friendly waitress met us shortly after we sat down, gathered our trays, checked what we were drinking, and asked if we'd need any steak sauce. Within a few minutes, one of the guys from the grill delivered our orders. They remembered who had ordered what and placed the plate in front of the right person. The first bite of steak was tremendous—I quickly knew this would be the first of many trips to eat there.

In 1966, Gus and Kasiana Aslanidis were looking for a better life for themselves and their four children. They left their tobacco farm in rural Greece and moved to the

United States where they initially worked with family in the restaurant business. Within a few years, they opened a steakhouse of their own called G&D Family Steakhouse.

G&D quickly became routine—nearly every Wednesday and always after church on Sundays. Gus and Kasi were similar in age to my parents and always friendly, asking about family, friends, and how classes were going. Their sons, Alex and Angelo, quickly became good friends. Within a few visits, I knew that if I was going to catch up with Angelo, it might not be at the grill. His wife, Elly, would send me to the cooler or prep kitchen in the back, where Angelo was cutting steaks. We talked politics, sports, business, family, the news, and more. These discussions were deep and personal. It was more than a visit with a friend—I had a true connection with the Aslanidis family. They embraced Beth as one of their own, too.

The summer before Beth and I were married, I ate at G&D nearly every day, enjoying the special, their gyro, or the chopped steak sandwich. When I asked them to fix the chopped steak on Texas toast instead of a bun—and to add extra garlic and onions—they nicknamed it "the Brand burger." It's never officially appeared on the menu, but I've had friends go in, introduce themselves, and order it by name. It remains one of my favorites to this day.

A trip to G&D meant more than a good meal; seeing the Aslanidis family was the highlight. After our honeymoon, the first place Beth and I went was G&D. Angelo's boys, Gus and Michael, would often sit with us as we enjoyed our meal, and nearly every visit included Angelo or Alex pulling up a chair and joining us at the table for a visit. After our first child was born, we didn't go straight home— we went to G&D so they could meet the newest member of the family. Through the years, we've taken family and friends to G&D countless times and met others there for reunions. We celebrated our son-in-law's graduation there, and, more than twenty years after introducing the Aslanidis family to our first baby, we found ourselves back again to introduce them to the next generation with our first grandson.

Today, the visits aren't as frequent as the years in college or when we lived in Jefferson City, but every minute there is special. We enjoy catching up with Alex, visiting with Elly and Angelo, and seeing their son Michael and his family continuing the tradition—greeting customers, preparing food, and making everyone feel at home.

The quality of the food at G&D has always been exceptional—but it's the connection with the Aslanidis family that makes it worth the trip every time. Sometimes, family isn't about blood or DNA. Sometimes, it's the love found in friends who welcome you like one of their own.

A familiar table, a cherished friend—one of many visits with Angelo Aslanidis at G&D Steakhouse in Columbia, Missouri.

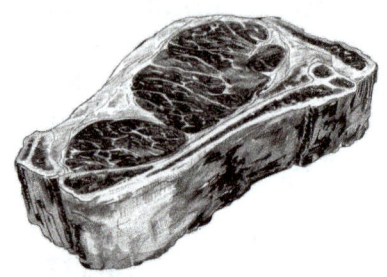

Ask anyone who's been through the doors of G&D: the experience starts before you even sit down.

The grill's just inside the entrance—a sizzling welcome that sets the tone. You grab a tray, pick up your silverware, and walk past the crew—always friendly, always focused. It's not just dinner; it's choreography. The orders go in without a notepad, and somehow, the steaks land at your table perfectly cooked and perfectly placed. Small magic. Every time.

But the real magic? That's in the back kitchen.

That's where I found myself again and again, watching Angelo cut steaks—sleeves rolled up, rhythm steady. The smell of steak in the air, the hum of the meat cutter, and then his voice:

"Tommy, you're like family to me."

You can't fake that kind of welcome. You can't franchise it. I already felt like family, but hearing him say it—that went straight to the heart. I think of his words every time I see him. Our hugs are genuine. When I say, "Love you, buddy," he always answers, "Love you, too."

Very few people call me Tommy. But Angelo does, and I don't mind. It's a reminder he's my family. His Greek accent makes me wish I could speak the language, too.

G&D isn't flashy, and it doesn't need to be. The menu doesn't change. The people don't, either. That's the secret. It's not just what's on the grill—it's who's behind it.

Every visit is steady and warm—a reminder that consistency is its own kind of excellence. And that sometimes, the best meals aren't about what's on the plate, but who you share them with.

And if you're lucky, someone in the kitchen still hollers, "Tommy's here!" when you walk through the door.

DANCING IN THE KITCHEN

One might describe the scene as a whirlwind. The timer beeps, signaling it's time to pull the rolls from the oven. On the counter lie the remnants of what was once a beautiful turkey, its golden skin now stripped away. The kitchen table is filled with dishes replicated on the dining room table. At the refrigerator, a container is refilled with ice cubes, while my sister opens a drawer to grab another serving spoon. A little one dashes through the crowd, tugs at my pant leg with her beautiful smile, silently asking for a taste of cheese—or whatever is nearby. I've learned she prefers something sweet.

There's room for double the number of people in the kitchen, but it's not yet time to welcome the crowd to the kids' table. The storm of Thanksgiving is brewing, and Mom tells one of us to start gathering everyone at the dining room table, knowing it will take several minutes to get their attention and for them to take their places.

Amid the frenzy, at the most inappropriate time, I grab my mother's arm and ask a question I heard my dad ask hundreds of times through the years: "Do you want to dance?" It was a question he asked in the midst of mayhem as well as when we were having fun. I know it's the last thing Mom wants to hear—and the last thing she wants to do—but she'll oblige, let me grab her, and dance just a few steps to pause from the commotion. It's a wonder she hasn't socked me at least once through the years. Instead, she indulges me, letting me twirl her around, however briefly.

That dance, however brief, always makes me pause and take in the moment. It's a reminder that, amid the frenzy, the heart of Thanksgiving is about the people around you and the memories you create together. Every family has its own traditions—some loud and boisterous, others quiet and subtle. For us, it's always been about the little things: who's cutting the cheese and arranging it in a unique pattern, the playful declarations about who sits where, the familiar

59

dishes that make their way to the table year after year, using Mom's "good dishes," and even a quick dance in the chaos.

And then, as everyone finally gathers around the table, the chaos fades into laughter, the clinking of serving spoons in dishes, and heartfelt thanks for the abundance in front of us—and around us.

I imagine scenes like this take place in homes all across the country, each with its own unique flavor and cast of characters. Yet the way the day unfolds is strikingly similar—families gathered around tables, sharing food and laughter, and taking a moment to give thanks for the abundance we're blessed with every day.

> "We should consider every day lost on which we have not danced at least once."
> — FRIEDRICH NIETZSCHE

For as long as I can remember, Mom's "good dishes" made an appearance at all the family holiday meals—Easter, Thanksgiving, and Christmas. They aren't fancy compared to china you'd buy today in a department store, but they were special to us—a Currier & Ives pattern collected piece by piece when Mom bought groceries, back when stores rewarded loyal customers with a plate or bowl tucked into the sack. Over the years, Mom added more: some gifted from Aunt Marie when she "retired" her set, others found at auctions or garage sales. Today, there are enough place settings to cover the kitchen table, the dining room table, and the extra tables set up in the living room, plus several matching serving dishes.

In recent times, there have been suggestions about switching to paper plates and plasticware to make cleanup easier. But Mom has stood firm—and most of us are glad she has. A paper plate might carry the food, but only the "good dishes" carry the years with them.

THE CAT THAT CAME AT CHRISTMAS

Growing up on our farm, we never had much luck keeping a cat. It seemed like roaming tomcats or a misjudged dash across a driveway kept us from having one for long. One of my earliest memories involved a cat—but it wasn't a good experience. Unprovoked, an old tomcat on the farm scratched me across the face, leaving a scar I carry to this day. Despite that, I still liked cats—thanks in large part to Grandpa Alexander.

Grandpa had a knack for keeping cats around. I remember tagging along with him to the granary at the end of the garage, where he kept their food. The sound of an old coffee can scooping Meow Mix and the clink as it hit the hog pan is vivid even now. That granary had its own charm, with the sweet smell of molasses lingering from the horse feed stored there. Watching Grandpa care for those cats and seeing their personalities probably sealed my lifelong affection for them.

The early winter of 1981 was a cold one in northwest Missouri. Frozen hog waterers and pilot lights going out seemed like a constant battle. That year, our family was about to have an unexpected guest who would brighten those long, cold months.

It was Christmas Eve, and chores were done for the morning. I was inside helping Mom when there was a knock at the front door. When I opened the door, there stood our school superintendent, Bob Kelley, cradling a young kitten. Mostly white, with some black and gray markings. Mr. Kelley knew how much I wanted a cat and offered the kitten as a Christmas present.

Because of the bitter cold, we decided the kitten would stay in the mudroom. With its small propane stove, space for a litter box, and enough warmth to stay cozy, it was the perfect spot. We named him Kelley in honor of the man who brought him. Though we expected him to move to the barn come spring, Kelley quickly became part of the family.

Kelley was a constant source of entertainment. In the evenings, he'd join us in the living room. My brother and I built him a "kitty condo" out of leftover Christmas boxes—complete with crawl spaces and living quarters. He never seemed to tire of the games, and neither did we.

Despite Mom's no-pets-inside rule, my brother Joe eventually decided Kelley might be more comfortable sleeping in his room. He tucked the litter box at the foot of the bed and snuck the kitten in. It wasn't long before Kelley became a regular in Joe's room—house cat privileges officially granted. The bitter winter dragged on, only strengthening the case for keeping him indoors.

As the weather warmed, Kelley settled into life as an indoor/outdoor cat. He'd meow at the door to go out, always preferring the outdoors to the litter box. But no matter how far he wandered, he always came back—a quiet reminder of how a small act of kindness on a cold Christmas Eve brought warmth to our family for years to come.

"If man could be crossed with the cat,
it would improve man but deteriorate the cat."

"A home without a cat—and a well-fed, well-petted,
and properly revered cat—may be a perfect home, perhaps,
but how can it prove title?"

— MARK TWAIN

The first time Kelley saw a mouse, he panicked, ran straight up Joe's coveralls, and clawed his way up Joe's face to his forehead. Fortunately, embarrassment is a great teacher. Kelley grew into a top-tier mouser, proudly delivering "presents" to the porch for Mom, who praised him with the same energy one uses when receiving an unwanted fruitcake. He also conquered the cast iron boot scraper shaped like a dog—after months of terror, Kelley finally slapped it silly and declared victory. After that, there was no living with him.

THE STAR ON THE SILO

Anyone who has traveled north on Highway 148 late at night or in the early morning hours knows the stretch beyond the 102 River bridge north of Pickering. The highway runs flat and straight, forcing tired drivers to remain alert as they near their destination. On cold winter nights, when the darkness is broken only by the occasional distant light, many have shared how comforting it is to see the familiar glow south of Hopkins. There, on the east side of the highway, perched atop a hill, stand two silos, the tallest nearly 100-foot-tall. Between Thanksgiving and Christmas, what sits atop that silo has been part of my family's story.

The farm was once known as the McCleave Place, though locals before that called it Hickory Hill, due to the hickory trees scattered throughout the grove and up to the house. It's the place I've always known as home, and that concrete silo predates my arrival in the early winter of 1971. Built by Turner Construction, the oblong structure with its honeycomb-shaped slabs became home to a star when I was in grade school. A 100-foot-long extension cord was dropped from the top, tied to the star, and the star was hoisted up, then fastened with baling wire to the circular safety ring on top. Adorned with 50 lights, the initial design included white bulbs with blue tips. A few years later, in an effort to give the star a bit of lift above the rings, legs were added to the base, raising the star higher and providing added stability.

Dad, brothers Bill and Joe, and eventually myself made the trek, along with grandkids, nieces, nephews, and even friends and neighbors. Bulbs—either burned out or broken off due to weather or the occasional bird that used one as a perch—needed replacing. Though the climb to the top is challenging, the view is magnificent. On a clear day, Mount Alverno to the south seems close, and Hopkins feels just a stone's throw away. I even remember hearing the chimes from the Christian Church on a calm day, when there was a gentle breeze blowing south.

When Turner Construction built the silo in the late 1960s, it represented progress for my dad's cattle-feeding operation. Though its original purpose has faded with time, the star on the silo has grown into something much greater: a testament to faith, family, and tradition.

Through the years, people have shared what the star means to them. For some, it's a welcome marker of being closer to home on a long, dark drive. For others, it's simply a comforting sight on a cold winter night. To many, the star atop the silo is more—it's a beacon of light and hope. Like the star in the east that guided wise men to Bethlehem to see a promised king, this star shines as a reminder of faith, proclaiming joy to the world. For decades, it has stood tall against the winter night, a symbol of home, family, and the promise at the heart of Christmas.

WONDER BREAD SACKS AND SNOW FORTS

The National Weather Service recorded an official snowfall total of sixteen inches from a weekend blizzard in early 2025, a figure that felt understated when paired with the howling winds and towering drifts that transformed the landscape into a snow globe. I remember plenty of heavy snowfalls in my life, and that one was a doozy! Even with the aid of the snowblower, clearing the drive, sidewalks, and a path through the yard for our postman took several hours.

There were multiple winters in the 1970s that packed a punch with both an abundance of snow and some bitter cold temperatures. Despite the depth of the drifts and the biting chill of those storms, I looked forward to snow days, uninterrupted Saturdays, and the chance to improve on past creations in the wintry landscape.

Preparing for outdoor adventures required careful planning. To stay warm, we'd pile on layers: long johns, t-shirts, a thermal shirt, a hooded sweatshirt, and coveralls for good measure. For our feet, the go-to method was wool socks tucked inside old Wonder Bread sacks, which then slid into shoes and finally into five-buckle boots. Mittens were always better than gloves, but on the coldest days, jersey gloves worn under mittens provided extra insulation. Topping off this ensemble was a stocking hat, a scarf, and a bandana tied snugly over the nose and mouth. I'm sure the resemblance to Ralphie from *A Christmas Story* was uncanny.

The challenge of getting dressed was only a divergence from the adventures that awaited in the Arctic tundra. After a thorough inspection of snow depths in different areas of the front and back yards, dragging the sleds from the machine shed for later use, and outlining the game plan, the work on projects could begin. Inevitably, we'd begin with a few snow angels. I was rarely satisfied with the results, as it seemed the footprints at the base distracted from the intended design.

Deep, long drifts on the north side of the house were the perfect location for tunneling. My brother Joe was a tunneling expert in the deepest areas and could transform an ordinary drift into a network of tunnels that rivaled any fort. Equipped with covered hands and occasionally an old ice cream bucket, he was the master engineer of our winter escapades, ensuring every tunnel had just enough room to crawl through without collapsing, and sometimes even adding "rooms" to our frosty hideaways.

When we'd grow cold, we'd retreat to the mudroom to shed snow-covered clothes and warm up. A cup of homemade hot chocolate in the kitchen, often paired with a sweet treat Mom had baked, made the return indoors just as memorable as the adventures outside.

These days, winter snow means firing up the snowblower, grabbing shovels, and checking road conditions. Occasionally, I toy with the idea of making a snow angel, burrowing into a drift, or constructing the walls of a snow fort. But those ideas quickly lose their charm when I consider the logistics of getting up from the frozen ground or the inevitable stiff-jointed regret that comes with crawling out of a snow fort at my age. Still, when I see the untouched snow, I can't help but admire the blank canvas, ready for the next set of memories yet to be created.

"Snow provokes responses
that reach right back
to childhood."
— ANDY GOLDSWORTHY

FIREWORKS ON INDEPENDENCE DAY

There's a sweetness to celebrating freedom.

It's not just in the fireworks or the parades—it's in the little things. The way hot dogs sizzle on the grill. The way potato salad somehow tastes better under a tree in Grandma's backyard. The way laughter and sparklers rise together into a summer night sky.

Growing up, Independence Day wasn't just a holiday. It was an event. We'd often head to Bedford, Iowa, for the parade, and we weren't just spectators—we were part of the lineup. For a few years, we rode with the Hopkins Saddle Club, making the ten-mile trek north on horseback to join the lineup. Horses were naturally placed at the end of the parade ahead of the street sweeper, so arriving too early meant letting your horse roast in the sun while the bands, floats, and convertibles did their thing.

Other years, we brought a different kind of horsepower. Our old 1954 Ford Business Coupe made its share of appearances, rumbling into town with Grandpa Alexander behind the wheel and Grandma riding shotgun. When I was little, I'd climb into the back—which wasn't really a seat at all, just open space where a young passenger could bounce around and wave at the crowd. Later, I drove the '54 myself—three on the tree, straight-six under the hood, and more character than anything out there today. In recent years, my best friend Kyle O'Riley has taken up the shotgun seat—still no air conditioning, but plenty of good stories between the parade route and the gas station snacks.

Most years ended the same way—with a backyard celebration at Grandma and Grandpa Alexander's. That's where the real magic happened.

The spread of food was everything a patriotic stomach could hope for. Burgers and hot dogs off the gas grill, potato salad chilled and waiting, baked beans bubbling in a slow cooker, and enough chips, dips, and deviled eggs to feed the entire township and then some. Grandma and

Mom were in charge of the table. Sometimes that table was a folding card table, sometimes a piece of plywood across sawhorses. Either way, it held the full bounty of the day.

And then there was the ice cream.

Our old electric maker had churned out more batches than I could count. The end of the motor's slow hum was the sign to unplug it—"before the motor burns up," someone always warned—and carefully lift out the beater. You let the cylinder sit in the salty slush for a while to firm up before scooping it into bowls. Grandma always had chocolate syrup and toppings ready, though honestly, that homemade vanilla needed no help.

When dusk finally—finally—settled in, it was time for fireworks. My brother Joe and I handled the lighting duties. It felt like the sun took its sweet time setting on purpose, just to test our patience. Grandma loved the fountains, so we always made sure to include a few for her. The grand finale was never choreographed or professional, but it was ours. Loud, colorful, chaotic. Perfect.

Dad had a line that always made us laugh, usually after a particularly brief burst in the sky: "That was pretty. What did that cost?"

And then, there were the peacocks.

Uncle Robert lived just across the field. Every time a bottle rocket popped, his peacocks would let out a screech in reply. You'd light a fuse, hear the firework whistle skyward—and immediately after, those birds would holler like they'd just been drafted. It was our own soundtrack of freedom, brought to you by livestock with flair.

The smells of Independence Day still come back to me, clear as ever. Grilled meat. The tang of mustard and vinegar in the salads. The sweetness of warm chocolate syrup melting into ice cream. And the unmistakable scent of fireworks—the faint sulfur and smoke of bottle rockets and roman candles, hanging like the aftertaste of celebration

We call it Independence Day because that's what it is. Not "the Fourth of July," not a date on a calendar—but a

68

reminder. Of risk. Of sacrifice. Of the vision of a people who believed liberty was worth the cost. And all across the country, in parades, backyards, and homemade ice cream bowls, we celebrate what came from that decision: the freedom to live, to gather, and to raise our families in peace.

That's what I think about when I hear the sizzle on the grill or the pop of a firework. I think about Grandma's backyard. About the parade route. About Dad's one-liners and peacocks gone wild. I think about how sweet freedom really is—and how lucky we are to taste it.

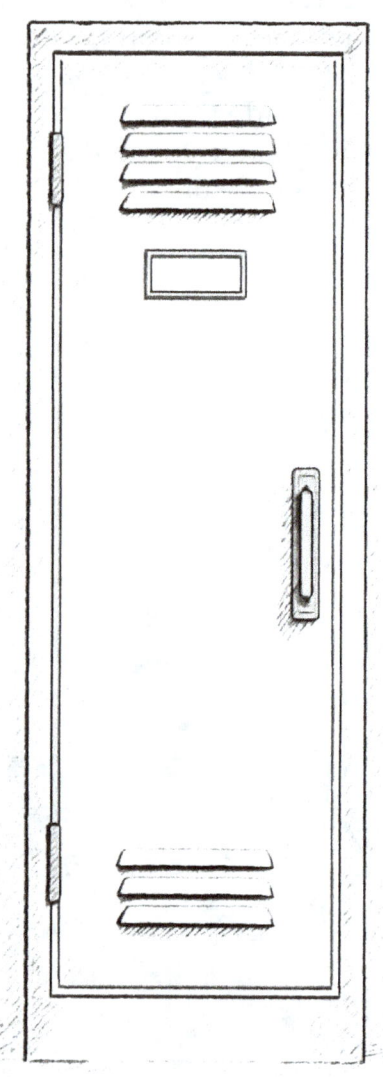

SCHOOL DAYS AND SHARP PENCILS

I didn't ace every test—but I remember the moments that mattered. This section holds memories from classrooms and competitions, typewritten games, and the gentle chaos of figuring out who you are before you know how to shave. Whether it was memorizing state capitals or buzzing in at the Brain Bowl, these stories shaped more than my GPA. They helped build the kid who loves a good story.

"The beautiful thing about learning
is that no one can take it away from you."
– B.B. KING

TAPED SHUT AND FULL OF CANDY

Every February in elementary school, red construction paper would appear on our desks, and the annual hunt for our safety scissors—last seen cutting out Christmas ornaments—would begin. Teachers demonstrated on the blackboard how to draw a heart, then supervised as we copied the design to the special paper. Once approved, each of us would carefully cut out the shape using two pieces stacked on top of each other, then we stapled them together, leaving the top of the heart open for the valentines that would be delivered in just a few days. The valentines were simple in design, filled with sweet messages appropriate for all my classmates, as well as the teacher. While I don't remember much about those valentines, I do remember the glue on the envelopes being poor and not wanting to stick closed, so we usually gave up and taped them shut.

As the years went on, the tradition evolved into a full-blown homework assignment where we were asked to get a shoebox, decorate it appropriately, cut a hole in the top, and bring it back to school on Valentine's Day. By this time, the valentines were a little larger, and many of my classmates also included a package of Brach's Conversation Hearts. It was nice to get a sweet treat, but today, I'd pass the package along to another in hopes of scoring a bit of Brach's chocolate instead.

When I was a student at North Nodaway, we transitioned to the Hopkins building in fifth grade, leaving Pickering behind. That's when we began switching classes throughout the day—just like the big kids. Fifth through eighth grade were mainly on the second floor, with the high school on the third floor of the building. Because of that integration, a lot of the activities were open to the entire student body.

The Future Homemakers of America (FHA) students sold flowers each February as a fundraiser. If I remember right, carnations were $1 each, and a rose could be ordered

73

for a premium price. The order forms let students choose what color flower to send to others. The colors represented different things: "I'm glad we're friends," "I want to get to know you," "I like you," or "I love you." I don't recall ordering a flower when I was in school—probably because I didn't have a steady until I was a senior in high school—but I do remember those FHA members staying busy throughout the morning with their flower deliveries. There were always a few students who were surprised to receive a flower, some who were disappointed they didn't, and others who blushed when their flowers were delivered.

That steady girl I was dating my senior year? I proposed a few years later, and we've been married since 1992—the sweetest sweetheart I could ever ask for.

I'm not sure when it started, but I've always liked a good card. Not the cheap ones, but the ones that feel right—the paper, the picture, the words that sound like somebody actually meant them. Picking the right card takes longer than I'll admit. So does saving them. I've got a stack tucked away—some for the memories, some for the handwriting, some because they just made me smile. I don't have every card Beth's ever given me, but I've kept a bunch—especially the Valentines, from the sweetest sweetheart a guy could ask for. They're in the top dresser drawer, mixed in with a few other things I couldn't stand to lose. The best ones weren't the fancy ones. They were the ones that showed up, same as she always has.

THE KMA BRAIN BOWL

Some kids dream of draining the game-winning shot in a packed gymnasium. I had a different fantasy: being part of the Brain Bowl competition on KMA Radio. Yes, I've always lived on the edge.

Back before I ever cracked a microphone professionally, I got my first taste of radio on KMA's Brain Bowl, a slightly unconventional academic competition that played out over the airwaves instead of under fluorescent gym lights. KMA—Shenandoah's pride and joy—was one of those rare radio stations that didn't just serve a community; it *was* the community. They had history. They had credibility. They had The Blackwood Brothers, The Everly Brothers, *Kitchen Klatter*, and a farm-and-homemaker lineup that would make any Extension office jealous.

And they had Bill Bone, a news director with a voice like velvet-covered authority. If you grew up in the KMA listening area and heard Bill, you knew it was news.

Our North Nodaway Brain Bowl team made the weekly 70-mile pilgrimage to Shenandoah to record our matches. We weren't in it for the glory. We weren't in it for the prize money. We were in it because we kept winning. The team—coached by our high school history teacher, Marvin Murphy—was stacked: Jared Wilmes and Lonny Graves were well-rounded trivia machines; Lorrie Morrison was a current-events and math wizard; and I, apparently, was there in case a question about state capitals or obscure historical trivia popped up.

The Brain Bowl had a unique format. If you answered a toss-up question correctly, you earned a set of three bonus questions. Nail all three, and not only did you rack up points—you shaved time off the clock. In academic bowl terms, that's like playing keep-away with the rulebook.

We advanced deep into the competition, eventually squaring off with a school—I wish I remembered which— that was giving us more trouble than a 10-point algebra question. We were behind, the clock was ticking, and I hadn't answered a single question. I was basically the mascot at that point.

Then it happened.

The moderator asked:

"How did the following people die? John Jacob Astor—"

I buzzed in before he even finished the sentence.

"North Nodaway—Brand," Bill Bone announced. (After all, this was radio—there was no live audience, just the sound of a name hanging in the air.)

My teammates turned to me with a mix of horror, disbelief, and the unspoken question:

Did Brand just go rogue?

Yes. Yes, I did. Because I knew something they didn't: John Jacob Astor went down with the Titanic. I didn't need the rest of the list. I didn't need context. I just needed to say two words, delivered with the conviction of someone who'd read every Titanic book in our school library:

"They drowned."

Correct.

We got the bonus questions. We answered all three. We won the match by just a few points—points that only came because of that answer and those bonus questions.

We advanced to the finals, where we faced Savannah, Missouri—reigning national champs. They were smart, fast, and ruthless. They didn't just beat us—they used us to mop the trivia floor. But hey, second place isn't bad when you were nearly eliminated and got saved by a fact about a Gilded Age millionaire who couldn't swim.

The Brain Bowl didn't make us famous, but it gave us a taste of competition, a reason to road-trip to Shenandoah, and in my case, one glorious moment of academic heroism that I will absolutely continue to milk for the rest of my life (and yes, I still know my state capitals).

PROJECT RMS TITANIC

Before Leonardo DiCaprio ever shouted "I'm the king of the world," before *Titanic* had an Oscar, a billion-dollar box office, or Celine Dion's soundtrack going on and on—I was already hooked.

The fascination started when news came across the radio Robert Ballard had found the wreckage of the *RMS Titanic* in 1985. But it was an article in *Newsweek*—with images and an interview with Ballard—that reeled me in. From that point on, I was a Titanic junkie. I read everything I could get my hands on.

At school, we had an Apple IIe in the library, and I started to code a text-based computer game: a *"Choose Your Own Adventure"*-style program about raising the Titanic. My brother Joe had access to a computer lab at Northwest Missouri State University, so he'd help input the long strings of code I scribbled out in pencil on college-ruled paper. I was a speedy two-finger typist, but Joe was faster.

The game offered the player multiple paths—each leading to a new storyline. Some led to success, others to disaster. A wrong decision delayed the mission, or you could run out of funding before even reaching the wreck. A wrong move in the salvage expedition could even end in death. It was a little like the *Oregon Trail* computer game, only without dying of cholera and completely taking place under water.

There were crude graphics, which felt pretty advanced for the time. I remember programming the descent to the Titanic with a top-down "view" of the wreck— just some blocky outlines and open funnel holes—which in my head looked like James Cameron concept art—but I was proud of it. While the program drew the holes where the ship's funnel had been, a message appeared: "Please wait as the deck comes into focus."

I poured over printouts of code and chased down bugs that caused endless loops or crashes. When I got stuck,

I knew I could turn to our high school math teacher and resident programming guru, Basil Lister, for help. He never let me down.

The grand finale, if you made all the right choices, was raising the ship. The image showed the cables growing shorter as the Titanic slowly lifted off the ocean floor—one painfully redrawn pixel at a time. Classmates and even teachers played it, sometimes as a group. Like Oregon Trail, the fun was in the decision-making…and trying not to get anyone killed.

Somewhere, on an old 5¼-inch floppy disk, a copy of the game might still exist. Whether it will boot up or not is anyone's guess. I'd like to think it's still out there—lines of *Applesoft BASIC* patiently waiting for a new player to try and bring the Titanic to the surface.

Spring always brings a quiet reminder: April 15, 1912—the night the Titanic slipped beneath the surface. More than 1,500 lives were lost in the icy waters of the North Atlantic. While my youthful fascination focused on the technology and drama of raising the ship, I've come to better appreciate the real cost behind that night. It wasn't just steel and steam that went down—it was stories, families, and futures. Remembering them is part of why the Titanic still rises in our collective imagination.

Some ships never truly disappear.

> In my opinion,
> the real treasure is not the shipwreck itself,
> but the stories it can tell.
> — ROBERT BALLARD

TRYING OUT FOR TRUMAN TIGER

The Antlers were the collegiate version of the basketball loud crowd at the University of Missouri in the 1980s. Dressed in black shirts with a large golden "A" adorned with antlers, they gained notoriety for taunting visiting teams and their coach, unleashing carefully timed signs as each opposing player was introduced. The crowd at the Hearnes Center would watch for their signs and shout along with them. The fifth player was always greeted with "smells like a bus!" Coach Norm Stewart loved the boisterous Antlers and knew their presence affected the opposing team. I wanted to be an Antler. But it wasn't in the cards for this kid from Hopkins.

Not becoming an Antler may have led to another opportunity I never dreamed of. The seed was planted the first week of my freshman year at Mizzou when I met an upperclassman named Dan Meers. His friendliness made a quick impression, and I learned he was Truman the Tiger, the university's mascot. Dan shared the process for becoming Truman, and we kept connected throughout the school year.

In the spring, an ad in *The Maneater* campus newspaper invited students to audition for Truman. The informational session outlined what would be involved, and a plan began to come together. I called Mom and Dad for suggestions, and they reminded me of a great resource. My former third grade teacher, Shirley Kelley, and school superintendent, Bob Kelley, had a son in Columbia who was in the fine arts program. Roger's talents as a performer and choreographer were just what was needed, so I called and asked for his assistance. Roger, who could've choreographed a Broadway number using only yard tools and optimism, helped me design a routine that included a Jimmy Durante song, a malfunctioning jambox that could only be fixed when Truman hit it with his cane, and an oversized golden yo-yo decorated with a tiger paw on the side.

The largest challenges were dealing with the limited view from inside the suit, trusting Truman's oversized head would actually stay put through all the antics, *and* keeping up a high energy level. The tryout went well, despite my exhaustion and the excessive amount of sweat from dancing and running around for the routine.

Following the audition, a panel of judges from the sports marketing department interviewed all the candidates. They asked the usual, "Why do you want to be Truman?" but one question stuck with me: "If you could be anything on the McDonald's menu, what would you be—and why?" I said, "The fries—because everyone loves the fries."

They must've liked the answer. Or maybe they just appreciated a performance that involved choreography, audio malfunctions, and a tiger swinging a golden yo-yo to the sound of Jimmy Durante. Who's to say?

There were four Trumans chosen out of a group of over 30 students. For the next three years, I wore the suit at alumni events, gymnastic meets, parades, elementary schools, wedding receptions, and several basketball games. Every basketball game included a little time with the Antlers and their crazy antics. I was fortunate to be one of the Trumans, representing Mizzou anonymously as an individual, but always as one of the most recognizable figures loved by young and old fans.

I never became an Antler. But I did something better—I got to dance, spin my tail, wave, and occasionally sweat through the layers while kids gave me high-fives and grown men shouted "Go Tigers!" at a mascot who couldn't answer. It turns out, you don't have to shout from the stands to make some noise. Sometimes, all it takes is a busted jambox, a golden yo-yo, and a tiger suit.

THE 'M' IN MIZZOU

March had arrived, and with it, the season of madness. As usual, the Big Eight Conference was tough, with half the teams nationally ranked. The Missouri Tigers had climbed as high as sixth in the nation but stumbled in their final three games, losing to unranked Kansas State and Oklahoma. The season regular season finale was a loss to third-ranked kansas in larryville. (Yes, I intentionally spelled those with lowercase letters, as any self-respecting, chickenhawk-despising Tiger fan would.)

Home during college was the Christian Campus House, and of the seventeen guys in the house, there was a core group of us who had enjoyed multiple exciting seasons together watching the Tigers at the Hearnes Center. We committed to going to the Big Eight Tournament in Kansas City that spring but were unsuccessful in securing tickets from the Mizzou student allotment. Colorado, however, had an abysmal season, so we grabbed six tickets from their allotment. Six was the key number; six of us were committed Tiger fans. Six is also the number of letters it takes to spell **MIZZOU**.

Who knows what sparked the idea—maybe it was sheer school spirit, maybe it was just the adrenaline of a big game—but somehow, we decided our chests would become the ultimate fan canvas. *M-I-Z-Z-O-U*, painted bold and proud. Sitting together in the packed arena, we were bound to land on TV—because really, what were the odds six other guys had the same brilliant—and slightly questionable—idea for a mid-winter basketball game? I took the M, Kent claimed the I, Joel and Chris doubled up on the Zs, Scott rounded things out with the O, and Jimmy brought it home with the U.

Imagine the disappointment when we got to Kemper Arena and were directed to our seats two rows from the top. The players on the court for the first game were just slightly larger than ants. There was no way the television cameras would even see us here, as the font size would have been too small. Our shirts stayed on, and we were certain they would likely stay on when the Tigers took the court.

One of the geniuses in our delegation must have had some insight into how poor our ticket location was, as he packed binoculars to watch the games. This proved to be our secret weapon, though, as he scanned the crowd behind the Tiger bench for open seats. We were delighted to spot four openings in the section six rows behind the players' bench. Another two were just a few rows down in the same section.

Down the steps we headed to our new seats! No one asked to see our stubs, so we easily made our way to a prime location only minutes into the game. While unable to display our "full Mizzou," I peeled off my shirt, we shuffled places, and Jimmy stood next to me. If M-I-Z-Z-O-U couldn't make an appearance, at least we could show our support with an M-U spelled out.

Iowa State, whom the Tigers had squeaked out a four-point win against earlier in the season in Ames, was a formidable opponent. It was a tough battle, down to the final seconds, but a Tiger victory was just out of reach. We left Kemper in a glum mood with a two-and-a-half-hour return to Columbia ahead of us.

It was late when we got back to the house in Columbia. As I walked into my room, the message light on my answering machine was blinking. I hit 'play' and heard a familiar voice: "I guess you were at the game tonight. I saw you on TV. I'm sure you're *real* proud of yourself." The voice was my mom. She was right—I was real proud of myself! But I would have been even prouder if the Tigers had won the game.

SIX LETTERS, ZERO REGRETS

Of the six guys who proudly spelled "MIZZOU" across their chests that night at Kemper, four of us were farm boys from northwest Missouri—Mound City, Union Star, Grant City, and Hopkins. We came from places where Friday nights meant football and gravel roads, but college gave us something else: a new kind of bond. And there's something about the friendships you form in those years—especially when you live under the same roof—that go deeper than even the ones from home.

We've all taken different paths since. A circuit court judge. A farmer. An electrician. A guy who runs his own lawn care business. And yet, when I look at that photo—six college guys, shirtless, grinning like idiots with "MIZZOU" scrawled across our chests—I remember exactly what it felt like to believe that showing up that way meant something.

And for the record? We didn't use body paint.

We used markers.

Yes. Permanent markers.

Because apparently we had zero common sense.

In hindsight, it explains a lot. Had we used actual paint, we would've made a smeary mess under our shirts. But markers? They held. Too well. A friend recently reminded me—and backed it up with photographic evidence—of the frantic postgame effort to scrub ink from our skin like we were removing a bad decision (which, technically, we were). I thought college was supposed to *educate* us...

As for kansas (still lowercase), I didn't arrive at Mizzou with hatred in my heart—just healthy indifference. But it didn't take long. By the time I became Truman the Tiger, the rivalry had sunk in deep. Coach Norm Stewart famously refused to spend a dime in Lawrence. I took that a step further: I've never even set foot within the city limits.

The closest I ever came was coaching 8-man junior high football for St. Joseph Christian. We had a game in Lawrence—*technically*. But the field was outside the city limits. I stayed true. Drove through. Never stepped out. And certainly never opened my wallet.

Beth might say my distaste once bordered on irrational. I admit there was a time when even spotting that fabled bird on a license plate frame would set me off. I've calmed down. A little. I now tell people I allow up to five chickenhawks in my life. A generous cap, honestly.

But rivalries fade. Markers eventually come off. Games end. What stays is the memory. The friendships. And the story of six guys who—armed with nothing but bad ideas and black Sharpies—believed that spelling out "MIZZOU" in permanent ink made them part of something bigger.

And, in some ridiculous way... it did.

> "What we remember from childhood
> we remember forever—
> permanent ink, if you will."
> — CYNTHIA OZICK

FFA CONTEST

Each spring, the signs are unmistakable: deeper green grass in the yard, squirrels darting across the street, and the steady hum of lawn mowers in the neighborhood. And for students in agricultural education, these are also signs that FFA competition season has arrived.

Since its establishment in 1928, FFA—formerly known as the Future Farmers of America—has organized competitions among members. These contests have evolved over time and were rebranded as Leadership and Career Development Events (LDEs and CDEs), adapting to the changing landscape of career opportunities. In Northwest Missouri, LDE and CDE competitions are typically held throughout March and April at various host sites, including high schools and university campuses.

Dick Baldwin was my high school FFA advisor. He put a lot of time and effort into preparing students for competition, whether it was soil or livestock judging, poultry evaluation, or milk products. He was well-versed in nursery/landscape, floriculture, farm management, and all of the other contests. Mr. Baldwin understood how to give us the experiences and tools to make us competitive. Inside and outside the classroom, we pored through countless test examples and flipped through pages of reference sheets under his guidance. Continued practice was key to our success.

The speaking contests resonated with me. As a freshman greenhand, I competed in Creed Speaking. As a senior, I went the route of Prepared Public Speaking. Mr. Baldwin had me recite that speech in front of my classmates, at chapter meetings, to school faculty, at the Community Club, to my family, and in front of a mirror. I thoroughly knew that speech. It was about water quality, and there are sections I can still recite today, including the opening: "The day is hot, and you've been working up a sweat putting up hay. What's the best thing to cool you down? A tall, cold glass of water."

The experience of being on a contest team offered wonderful lessons. While each of us was judged individually, our cumulative score determined whether we qualified for the state competition. We didn't just study for ourselves—we studied together and challenged each other to improve. Through that process, each of us continued to grow and built our team-building skills along the way. Those skills were even more powerful than the individual knowledge we gained.

Looking back, I'm grateful for the invaluable experience gained from participating in FFA contests— lessons in teamwork, discipline, public speaking, and personal growth. Every spring, thousands of students and their advisors bring months of preparation into these competitions, growing both as individuals and as teams. Here's to them—and to the lifelong skills these contests help cultivate.

> I believe in the future of agriculture,
> with a faith born not of words but of deeds—
> achievements won by the present
> and past generations of agriculturists;
> in the promise of better days through better ways,
> even as the better things we now enjoy
> have come to us from the struggles of former years.
> — The FFA Creed, by E.M. TIFFANY

ONE WORD ON THE BACK: SECURITY

I was the bodyguard before Kevin Costner.

April 23, 1991. It was a Tuesday. I remember it well.

I was getting ready for my shift at the Hearnes Center on the University of Missouri campus. By then, I'd been working there for a little over a year. What started as a way to earn some side money had grown into something more—I'd been promoted and now served as head of student security for concerts and events. When I first started, the basic uniform was simple: khaki pants and a yellow T-shirt with one bold word across the back: **SECURITY**. With the promotion, I'd graduated to a collared shirt with the embroidered Hearnes Center logo and the MU shield on the front. I looked even more official now.

That night was another concert—part of the routine by that point. I'd already worked shows for New Kids on the Block, the Statler Brothers, George Jones, Conway Twitty, MC Hammer, Alan Jackson, and plenty of others. My boss, a former cop named Roger Crumpton from St. Joe, had taken a liking to me. I'd proven I could stay focused when the lights came up and the music got loud, and he trusted me with more responsibility.

Before every show, we met with the team and made assignments. You had to know who was working—who could be trusted to hold the stage line, who could manage entrances, who'd stay focused when the crowd surged. The biggest guys went to the front of the stage. The reliable ones? They guarded the restricted doors. I made the rounds, checked in, filled gaps, and kept things running.

But this night was different. Before the show, a small group of us from Hearnes met with the artist's head of security. And this guy? He took over immediately. He warned us—flat-out—that anyone caught watching the show would be fired on the spot. He meant it. I could tell. I passed that warning to the rest of the crew, word for word.

The stage was six feet high. We were short-staffed, so I took the front thrust of the stage—the narrow platform that extended into the crowd on three sides. If someone was going to try to get on stage, it was going to be right there.

Once the concert started, the artist came out and hit that thrust stage over and over. At one point, she leaned down, sang in my ear, and accepted a rose from someone in the audience. The crowd screamed. The lights flashed. And I never flinched. I stayed locked in the entire time, eyes scanning, posture steady. Despite my front row seat, I never saw her perform. Not once. I never looked at the stage.

After the final song, her head of security came over and shook my hand. He thanked me for doing my job.

That artist, by the way, was Whitney Houston

I was the bodyguard before Kevin Costner.

After the show, when I was off the clock, I walked up the tunnel leading into the Hearnes Center where Whitney Houston's tour bus was parked. A couple of guys I knew were on duty, so I stopped to visit.

The window to Whitney's bus was open. From where we stood, we could see her inside, fanning herself, taking a moment to catch her breath and some fresh air.

Out in the roped-off crowd, a little boy was hollering, calling out a name that caught Whitney's attention. She leaned out the bus window, turned to me, and asked if I could bring the boy over so she could visit.

I lifted him up and let him stand on my shoulders while he talked with Ms. Houston. He smiled. She smiled, and the conversation went on for quite a while. When he was finished, I let him down, and he slipped back behind the barrier, still grinning.

Whitney turned to me, thanked me, and asked if there was anything I needed. I pulled a tour poster from my back pocket—the one showing all the backstage passes from the night—and asked if she would sign it. She did, writing, "All my love, Whitney."

All these years later, I still have that poster—a reminder of being the bodyguard before Kevin Costner...and of the kindness Whitney showed a college kid in a security shirt.

THE LAST ONE HOME

Each fall, students settle into new routines—alarm clocks ringing earlier, bus stops shifting, backpacks heavier than common sense. Teachers grade homework, custodians sweep and clean at a hurried pace compared to the summertime, and lunchroom cooks are learning which students prefer the bread-and-butter sandwich made with heels instead of the standard slice of bread. Another essential part of the school day—one who should never be overlooked—is the school bus driver.

Like my sister and brothers before me, I caught the bus by the railroad tracks at the highway. For part of my kindergarten year, the bridge going to the Karl Richard Coleman place still existed, so Mike and Tim waited with us for the arrival of the familiar yellow International. With the elementary school in Pickering, I waited for the southbound bus while my brother Joe and the Colemans caught the northbound bus to Hopkins.

And that yellow International? It was driven by Glenn Owens, my first school bus driver. Dad had told me I'd probably get home ahead of Joe and wait for him at the railroad tracks by the highway. To my surprise, after the first day of school, Glenn didn't just stop at the highway. He pulled off, drove up the gravel road, then turned again—up our long lane—finally stopping right at the house. I thought I was a big deal! Dad noticed the special drop-off and told me to let Glenn know I could walk from the highway. Not wanting to miss out on a good thing, I waited to tell Glenn until he had already turned off the highway the next day. Up the driveway we went once again! At supper, Dad told me he'd run into Glenn in town and cleared up what I hadn't told him. From that point forward, I walked the lane—or, when conditions permitted, across the pasture—to get home.

The majority of miles I covered on the bus were with Maurice Riley behind the wheel. Those daily miles to and from school added up quickly over the years, but Maurice also drove us to most football games from junior high through high school. Always encouraging, he helped set the tone en route to the games and handed out compliments to everyone as they boarded the bus afterward, win or lose. I think it could easily be said that Maurice Riley was loved by all who rode his bus.

We had a great crew of bus drivers at North Nodaway. In addition to Glenn and Maurice, I rode the route with Danny Gamel and Lloyd Minshall. Each one had the respect of the students on board, no matter the age. Sure, there were times they'd glance in the mirror and holler at someone to settle down—and even a time or two when they'd pull over and hand out some discipline, old-school style.

Always ensuring the safety of their passengers, the bus driver is the last to reach home, dropping off every student along the way. Thanks to all the men who took me to and from school, ball games, track meets, and field trips all those years!

THE SUMMER 71 HIGHWAY CAME TO HOPKINS

Sometime in early 1986, the announcement came: 71 Highway was going to be rerouted through Hopkins for the summer. The detour would turn north of Maryville onto Highway 148, taking travelers through Pickering and Hopkins before continuing to Bedford, then west on Highway 2 to rejoin 71 in Clarinda. Along with the announcement came news that O'Riley Oil would be staying open later in the evenings to accommodate the extra traffic. That was music to my ears—because it meant an excuse to spend more time with friends.

Among those friends was Tony O'Riley, the owner's son, who would be working most evenings at the station. Despite having driven for years, I was still shy of my sixteenth birthday and couldn't legally drive to town. But with football season coming up, I figured jogging or biking the two-and-a-half miles into Hopkins could double as off-season conditioning. Once the chores were done and supper finished, I'd head north to hang out with Tony, Scott Swaney, and others who might drift by for an evening of storytelling, laughter, and the occasional gas pump duty.

Dad often shared stories about growing up in Hopkins and the cast of characters that filled his youth—tales of Deanie Cross' army, swimming in the 102 River, and wild rides with Harlan Lock and "Bad Boy" Neu. The adventures with Wayne White alone could fill a novel. His stories painted vivid pictures of a time before mine, filled with names I'd either had the privilege to meet or could clearly imagine. They were better than any book I'd read—because he made them feel real. After all, who doesn't love a good story?

Like so many small towns, friendships in Hopkins ran deep and wide. Because of those friendships, I was lucky to have an arsenal of my own stories. That summer, jogging

91

or biking to town added new chapters to my personal memoir. Tony was there each night. Scott, too. Both were upperclassmen who looked out for me and gave me a ride home so I wouldn't be on the highway after dark. People from the community would stop by to top off their tank, grab a candy bar, or just swap stories. We stayed out of mischief and enjoyed each other's company—and the company of whoever else came through. Compared to the legendary tales Dad told, our adventures may not have been as grand, but those nights deepened friendships and carved out memories from a summer when Hopkins sat a little more prominently on the map.

If a time machine ever becomes a reality, one of the first stops I'd make would be those summer nights at the filling station in 1986—spending time with friends, swapping stories, and adding new chapters to the novel of my life.

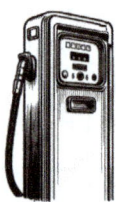

"Fill 'er up" is a phrase you don't hear much anymore. But back then, at O'Riley's, that's how most evenings began. A car would roll over the hose, ringing the bell inside, and Tony was already heading out—fuel cap off, nozzle in hand. If they came inside, the locals would grab a pop, tell a joke, and give us boys a little grief.

There was no AC, just a few worn-down chairs—surprisingly comfortable—good company, and the occasional slap boxing match. Swaney had both the size and reach on me, but I kept coming back—all in fun.

We didn't realize how special that summer was. We just knew the pump lights stayed on a little later—and so did the conversations.

No one ever wrote a song about Highway 71 coming through Hopkins.

But maybe someone should've.

VARM'T HUNTIN'

Why is it that sparrows are always the first at the bird feeder after it's freshly filled? Like pushy buffet-goers, they hog more than their fair share, shooing away the real VIPs—those colorful little finches, cheerful robins, and my personal favorite, the regal cardinals. The finches and friends? They're left to settle for scraps, pecking at what the sparrows have tossed to the ground like picky toddlers picking peas off their plates. And then there are the starlings—loud, obnoxious, and bringing more trouble than joy. Honestly, has anyone ever called a sparrow or a starling their "favorite bird"? I'd bet not. So when the chance came to join a varmint hunt to thin the flock, you'd better believe I was all in.

In the broad sense, "varmint" is the informal way to describe those wild animals that are a nuisance or pest. Who wants to go "nuisance pest hunting?" That makes it sound like a formal, English countryside outing. Varmint huntin' has a broader appeal—and it's far more fun to say, especially with a bit of a Northwest Missouri accent (properly pronounced, that's *varm't huntin'*).

Our ag advisor, Dick Baldwin, masterfully put together a scoring system for the chapter varmint hunt each year. Coyotes were worth the most points, with raccoons close behind. Squirrels, rats, opossums, skunks, and other four-legged troublemakers made the list. I mention "four legs" because to get your points, you had to bring in all four. Also on the list—those sparrows and starlings!

Equipped with my trusty Daisy BB gun, I could collect a few points each day around the barn and farrowing houses. But without a driver's license, I didn't do much varmint huntin' unless I tagged along with upperclassmen. That changed my junior year when some younger guys joined in. To say they were gung-ho would be an understatement. The posse included both Cassavaugh brothers, Chad and Keith, along with Steven Brown and Adam McIntyre.

These guys understood the assignment. They knew plenty of places to go—old barns where birds roosted at night and raccoons partied around the foundations. They brought gunny sacks and were armed with BB guns, tennis rackets, nets, and spotlights. We'd unload from the truck, quietly approach the barn, and begin the hunt, posting a man or two at the exits (properly equipped, of course) while the rest flushed the sparrows and starlings. We swung, lunged, and collected our prize eliminations. We rarely used the BB guns, though, as barn owners were quick to remind us not to put holes in the tin roofs.

Looking back, I'm sure we resembled the crews Jerry Clower used to tell stories about—especially when it came to huntin' with his Uncle Versie Ledbetter. Did we win the varmint hunt contest? I don't think so. But the adventures and the pure fun we had are memories I'll always treasure. They come to mind every time I see any member of that crew—or any smug little sparrow on my bird feeder.

Me and Uncle Versie and the Ledbetters
had treed a big ol' coon up in a
persimmon tree, middle of the night.
Sent John up to shake him out.

He gets up there and yells down,
"He ain't no coon! It's a bobcat!"

Uncle Versie hollered,
"Well, knock him out, John!"

Then we heard a terrible ruckus—
branches breakin', John screamin',
and somethin' howlin' to beat the band.

John hollered,
"Shoot up here amongst us!
One of us has got to have some relief!"
— JERRY CLOWER, "Knock Him Out, John!"

ROLLER SKATING AT THE RINK

For two and a half dollars, a person was guaranteed sore legs and maybe a few blisters at the skating rink. Skate Country Roller Rink, north of Maryville, was the place to be on a Saturday night for kids from all over the area—and it delivered hours of entertainment.

I had plenty of early exposure to roller skating through church or 4-H parties and the occasional school field trip. While my skills only improved incrementally over the years, I eventually developed a decent sense of balance and control. Multiple trips to Skate Country brought more confidence, even if I never got fancy with my footwork. Still, the experience was always enjoyable—and it left behind memories that have stuck around all these years later.

After paying the admission fee and standing in line, it was off to the rental area to report your shoe size and pick up a pair of skates. That area had a very specific smell— leather, carpet glue, the lingering tang of disinfectant from skates recently returned, and hundreds of nervous feet. Skates in hand, we'd find a bench, lace up, and stash our shoes in a nearby bin.

Skaters circled the rink counter-clockwise while the familiar music of the day pumped through the speakers, lights shifting in sync with the beat. The soundtrack was part of the experience. Sometimes you heard a song for the first time at the rink. Other times, the right song made skating feel effortless.

Between laps, a few floor games broke up the routine. Limbo was never my strong suit, but I gave it a try every time—then watched the more flexible kids slide under that bar like it was nothing. Four corners, circle skating, and speed skating were also weekend staples.

There was no need for a clock. You just knew the night was winding down when the announcer called for a couple skate. Without a girl by my side, I'd head to the bench, pull off the skates, and slip back into my shoes. When returning skates, the routine was always the same: tuck in the laces, set them on the counter, watch the worker give them a quick blast of disinfectant spray, and see them disappear back onto the shelves.

There aren't as many roller rinks around today as there once were, but you can still find a few scattered across the map. Places like B&J Skating in St. Joseph have even seen new life in recent years with renovations and fresh management. Grant City Skating Center has been open for seasonal weekends as well, keeping the wheels turning for a new generation.

Though fewer rinks remain, their timeless appeal endures. Whether through speed skating or just moving to the music, the memories still linger—places like Skate Country continue to spin on, one lap at a time.

> "Skating has always kept me young...
> The freedom and expression,
> I really feel like it's a language
> when you get deeper
> into the cultures of skating
> for rhythm, period."
> — USHER

When our son, Alex, was only a few years old, our minister's family (the Raymonds) gave him a pair of bright yellow and blue Fisher-Price skates. They adjusted to fit your foot and even had a lock to keep them from rolling backward. Alex didn't bother with that for long. Pretty soon he was skating up and down the hallway, leaving a trail across the floor like he owned the place.

By three, he had a pair of oversized rollerblades from another family at church (the Kennedys). They were too big, but Alex didn't care—he just strapped them on and went. Frontwards, backwards, turning on a dime. Smooth as anything. Meanwhile, I was the guy who treated roller skating like an Olympic event in falling down. Watching Alex made it pretty clear: sometimes, the knack skips a generation. I was just get lucky enough to witness it.

DOLLAR NIGHT AT THE HARDIN

In the early morning hours of April 13, 1955, fire consumed the Rialto Theatre in Bedford, Iowa, destroying the 1913 structure and the neighboring Dr. J.F. Hardin building. Out of the ashes rose a new movie house: the Hardin Theatre. While the fire marked a turning point in Bedford's history, the story that stayed with me was personal. My dad, part of the construction crew building the new theater, once survived a harrowing accident—riding a steel girder 35 feet to the ground during a partial collapse. He walked away, and the theater still went up.

We were lucky to have a good selection of movie theaters: the Hardin in Bedford, the Tivoli and Missouri theaters in Maryville, the Caprice in Clarinda. At one time, there were drive-ins in both Maryville and Clarinda, too. I remember seeing E.T., Deathtrap, and the early Star Wars films at the Hardin. But by the mid-1980s, the Hardin had shifted to second-run movies for $1 on Sunday nights— and that's when it became part of my own story.

Dollar movies in Bedford became a winter Sunday tradition with friends—Kyle O'Riley, James Spalding, and whichever parent volunteered to drive us. We were too young to drive, but not too young to soak up the magic of the big screen. We'd sit in the front row, popcorn in hand, sipping our cold drinks, fully immersed for two hours in another world.

We saw everything. The hits—*Raiders of the Lost Ark*, *The Goonies*, *Short Circuit*, *Mannequin*, and *Footloose*. And then the unexpected—films like *Yentl*, *Gandhi*, or *That's Dancing!* They weren't what most boys our age sought out, but they broadened our horizons. We watched Barbra Streisand pass as a boy to pursue her faith. We learned about peaceful resistance from Ben Kingsley. We nearly fell asleep during old musical montages...until *Thriller*, *Singin' in the Rain*, and John Travolta pulled us back to life. I wouldn't know who Esther Williams was if it wasn't for *That's Dancing!*

The ride home was always a highlight—us recapping favorite scenes, critiquing the parts we didn't understand, and laughing the whole way back.

Today, the Hardin Theatre still stands—not as a cinema, but as the American Legion. I've stepped inside a few times since, and it doesn't take much to feel those Sunday nights come rushing back—laughter, popcorn, stories shared in the dark. But always, just behind the movie memories, is another scene I can picture just as clearly: a young man holding tight to a falling girder…and surviving. My dad's story is forever part of that place, just like mine.

When James Spalding was around, it wasn't if mischief would happen — just when. Kyle and I were no saints, but James? James had a way of turning a Sunday night at the Hardin Theater into an event. He and Kyle were cousins, born just days apart, and they'd been stirring up trouble since they were old enough to walk.

James never went anywhere without a rat-tail comb jammed into his pocket, always straightening his hair in case the right young lady came along. Spitballs? He was a master—could hit a target halfway across the theater with a drinking straw and a glob of paper. And candy darts? He figured out you could spear a Tart n' Tiny with a hot sewing pin and fire it like a rocket. But the crowning achievement? One night, he chewed up three empty popcorn bags—mine, his, and Kyle's—loaded the soggy mass onto his comb, and catapulted it right onto the projection screen. It stuck two feet up—and stayed there. Honestly, if the theater was still going today, that thing would probably still be stuck to the screen. A legend in his own lifetime.

98

FRIDAY NIGHT LIGHTS

There's something special in the air each fall. There's the banging rhythm of corn going through the head of the combine, the crisp mornings nudging out summer's warmth, and a little dust lingering in the wind. And then there's the sound that's unmistakable: the voice of the public address announcer, cheerleaders chanting and clapping, the pep band in full swing, a cowbell ringing somewhere in the crowd, and the pop of shoulder pads colliding on the field.

The lights are on, the field is lined, and fans in school colors fill the bleachers. Referees meet the captains at midfield. The game begins. No matter the team's record, family, faculty, and community members show up. They always do.

North Nodaway had a strong stretch of seasons in the early to mid-1980s. For me, every part of the game felt personal. My brother's class and the siblings of my own classmates filled out the roster. The Coleman boys—our neighbors across the 102 River—were the first I watched closely. Mike, tough as nails, held the line while Tim commanded the huddle at quarterback.

Bryan O'Riley, Steve Knorr, and Kent Porterfield had the kind of speed that made you sit up in your seat. Darin Colville had a kicker's leg and laser aim—he could split the uprights with consistency. Todd Gorman and Rodney Vance were as rugged as they come, with a touch of cowboy that kept them moving long after most would've called it a night. Linemen like Charlie Blake (who I swear had a full beard in junior high) opened lanes, held the line, and gave the backfield time to work.

The rivalries were fierce—Tarkio, Rock Port, South Holt, Nodaway-Holt. The conference was full of talent, and rarely did a game end in a blowout. The excitement that team generated was electric. It reached every hallway in the school and spilled over into every corner of the community.

For the first time in my young life, I wasn't playing pickup ball behind the bleachers—I was walking the sidelines, cheering with parents and boosters. That's when I knew I wanted to suit up, too.

Each fall, when another generation of players is introduced under the lights, I think of those Mustangs. Their example—their grit—still echoes. Win or lose, they remind us what it means to show up, stand together, and play like it matters.

Because it does.

"You boys were eight and ten years old last time Alabama was on top. That was before any of you were paying much attention to it. What are you doing here? Tell me why you are here. If you are not here to win a national championship, you're in the wrong place. You boys are special. I don't want my players to be like other students. I want special people. You can learn a lot on the football field that isn't taught in the home, the church, or the classroom. There are going to be days when you think you've got no more to give and then you're going to give plenty more. You are going to have pride and class. You are going to be very special. You are going to win the national championship for Alabama."

— BEAR BRYANT

WHAT IT WAS, WAS FOOTBALL

One of America's most admired actors and comedians, Andy Griffith, was famous for playing Sheriff Andy Taylor and country lawyer Ben Matlock. His characters gave us vivid memories—Andy and Opie solving life's dilemmas, or *Matlock* delivering closing arguments that won the case. But one of my favorite memories is Andy Griffith himself, describing a trip to a football game—without ever saying the word "football."

In 1954, he released a monologue called *What It Was, Was Football*. In it, a country preacher describes a trip to a college campus where he sees "a bunch of fellers a-playin' with a pumpkin." It reached number nine on the *Billboard* charts and remains a timeless classic.

My own football journey started on the playground with unorganized scrimmages, then moved to junior high, where I learned the fundamentals. I was a big kid—short on speed, better suited for the offensive line. I settled into the position of center. If Andy Griffith had described it, he might've said, "that feller grabbed ahold of that funny-lookin' little pumpkin, lifted it between his legs, and this other feller behind him grabbed it and started to run around, lookin' for someone else to hand it to or throw at."

As a freshman, we didn't win a single game. Nine games. Nine losses. Then Coach Mike Butt came to North Nodaway, sharpened our skills, and we started improving. We won two games the next year. The season after that, we finished 4–4, including a hard-fought win over Tarkio—our first in 37 years—and a goal-line stand against Nodaway-Holt that ended with a game-winning drive.

Our senior year brought a new challenge: eight-man football. Fewer players on the line, fewer in the backfield— but the expectations went up. If someone wasn't giving their best effort, everyone knew. Weaknesses were exposed fast—ours and our opponents'. The physical part of the game still mattered, but now the mental game mattered more. Teamwork became everything.

That focus paid off—we finished 7–2.

The year after I graduated, the team went all the way and won the state championship. Their success was built on the foundation we laid together, week after week, snap after snap.

Andy Griffith's monologue is timeless. I wouldn't change a word.

But if he'd wandered into Hopkins on a Friday night in 1988, I think he'd have written a follow-up.

He might've called it: *What It Was, Was Teamwork.*

Coach Butt knew how to turn boys into a team. Practices were tough—but they were fun, too. We rotated between the sled, barrel rolls, and Alabama drills. Then linemen went one direction, backs and receivers another. Once practice started, you didn't walk. You ran. And if you slacked? You ran more. It was instant accountability—to your team and your coach.

We'd push the sled until the whistle blew, then hop on while the next guy pushed us. Eventually, we were pushing two guys—sometimes three. Our necks disappeared, going straight from the bottom of our ears to our shoulders.

Barrel rolls were chaos and rhythm. When it clicked, it was a painful, perfect dance. I loved being paired with guys who gave it their all. Big guys like Scott Swaney and Rick Frampton made it look easy. Indian running taught endurance and unity. Fall behind, and everyone paid.

I once heard a speaker talk about finding joy in what you do. Those practices—exhausting as they were—brought us joy through brotherhood.

But Coach wasn't just about grit. He carved out time before games, had us sit with our eyes closed, and walked us through each play—teaching us to see success before it happened.

That's what Coach taught us.

And that's what it was.

RINGING IN THE NEW YEAR

I'd never seen anything like it—a glowing ball of light descending a tall building as a crowd on television counted down in rising excitement. The host, whom I recognized from a Saturday music show, led the countdown as the ball dropped. When it reached the bottom, a sign lit up in sync with Dick Clark: "Happy New Year!"

I wasn't very old, but it made an impression. I've stayed up to watch the ball drop every year since.

As a kid, New Year's Eve often meant a trip to the movie theater with Mom and Dad's best friends, Wayne and Martha White. There was always something family-friendly playing—Freaky Friday, The Shaggy D.A., or 101 Dalmatians. Back home, my sister Debbie, brother Bill, and the White kids, Kirby and Lori, would be hosting a party of their own. I looked forward to the day I'd get to host one myself.

We finished our basement around the time I was in fifth grade, the same year we started attending classes in the school building at Hopkins. As the holidays neared, I asked if a few friends could come over for New Year's. With some ground rules and a guest list cap, Mom and Dad agreed— and a new tradition began.

The plan was simple: pizza for supper, snacks and 2-liters to feed a small army, card and board games, and a stack of movie rentals from Movie Magic in Maryville. We rented a VCR to go with them. Other than the occasional trip upstairs for provisions, we stayed in the basement, which was probably for the best, considering the noise level. Because at times, it sounded like a freight train made of Mountain Dew and pizza.

After the midnight countdown, we'd fire up more movies, tell stories, and entertain ourselves with the usual mischief. Ghost stories always made an appearance—and always seemed to sync with the sound of floorboards creaking upstairs. Someone would check, only to find Mom and Dad asleep. This led to whispered speculation that the house was haunted.

Eventually, the sleeping bags came out, and the floor transformed into a patchwork of blankets and boys. The electric fireplace cast a flickering glow from its rotating log, and the night finally settled.

In the morning, we woke to the smell of breakfast—eggs, bacon, and Mom's blueberry pancakes. Parents would arrive. Sleeping bags were rolled up. And though we hated to see the fun end, we knew we'd be back together again in a few days at school.

The tradition carried through the rest of my school years. And every time I watch the ball drop in Times Square now, I think back to those simpler celebrations—fewer fireworks, less fanfare, but just as much joy.

Because even as traditions evolve, the heart of it all stays the same.

Childhood memories sneak up on you
when you least expect them,
like a wonderful game of hide and seek.

The sweetest friendships
are with people who knew
(and still see) the child in you.

Our most treasured moments
aren't always the big, important ones.
Sometimes it's just the smell of cookies
taking us back to an ordinary afternoon.

Remember the open expanse
of an unplanned snow day,
or a summer afternoon.

Walk in the footsteps
of your childhood self
and wonder at the beauty of all you see.

— LOVETOKNOW

VOICES THAT ECHO

You can still hear them, if you listen close enough. The shopkeeper who handed you a little extra, just in case. The professor who asked "why," not just "how." The dad who said "I love you"—and proved it every day in the way he lived.

These stories are about the people who raised us, taught us, welcomed us, and reminded us that what you say—and how you say it—can leave a mark that echoes far beyond your years. Their echoes shape who we are— and who we choose to be.

> "What you do
> has far greater impact
> than what you say."
> —STEPHEN COVEY

THINGS DAD SAID

A florist once remarked, "Fathers haven't the same sentimental appeal mothers have." While Mother's Day has been celebrated since the early 1900s, Father's Day didn't receive official national recognition until 1972, during the Nixon administration. And each year, it seems the ties, barbecue tools, humorous t-shirts, and coffee mugs disappear from store shelves just a little faster around Father's Day.

Fathers—or father figures—have shaped each of our lives. Through example, watching, listening, and working together, the influence of fathers is multi-generational. For me, Father's Day is another opportunity to reflect on my own father and remember the many things he shared and taught me.

When we were working on a project, it would have been easier and quicker for Dad to cut boards, hammer nails, or drive posts himself, but he knew the best way for us to learn was to try it ourselves. Too many times, I found myself beating a nail or sawing a board with everything I had, thinking it would make the task go faster. Dad gave sound advice: **Let the tool do the work.**" I've remembered that in recent years, and it's saved me a lot of energy.

At home, the mid-day meal was dinner, and evenings brought supper. As we gathered around the table for dinner, the familiar voices of Jim Ross and Craighton Knau on KMA broadcast markets, news, weather, and more. When Dad was trying to hear something specific, he'd say in a firm voice, "**Listen!**" Instead of telling us to be quiet or shut up, that one word was a gift that served me beyond the dinner table. Listening made me realize that whatever Jim or Craighton was talking about was important—and made a difference in our lives.

As the youngest of three boys, I often found myself in the gate-opening position in the cab instead of behind the steering wheel. But when the opportunity came to be the one backing up or working with equipment, instead of guiding with "Come on back," or some other expression, Dad would say, "**Easy. Easy.**" We've joked through the years that sometimes it was announced more forcefully, but thinking back, I now see it was his way of keeping our minds off the difficulty of the task and focused on the simplicity of it. It took the Eagles years later to put this advice into a song with *"Take It Easy."*

Our own children were recipients of Dad's wisdom, too. When it came time to leave after a visit and the kids would rather stay, Dad would ask if they had a good time. The answer was always an enthusiastic, "Yes!" This would cue Dad's response: "**You have to leave if you want to come back.**" The thought may sound silly, but its message always led to a smile from the kids as they shifted their focus to the next return visit to Grandma and Grandpa's house.

My recollections of Dad are limited only by available space—it would take more ink than you'll find on a tanker ship to share them all. The impact and influence he had will continue through the rest of my life, and hopefully carry on, just a little, with each generation.

It's funny how we don't always realize the things our dads said are still riding along with us—tucked into our everyday vocabulary like old tools in a familiar box. Years later, we find ourselves repeating them to our kids, or hearing them echoed back in some new variation. Some phrases fade. Others evolve. But every so often, a line comes out of our mouths, and we hear his voice in it. That's more than memory—it's presence. Beyond the heirlooms or handmade treasures, there's something lasting about the words we carry forward. A few sayings, a little advice... maybe that's one of the best ways we keep them close.

IT'S A GOOD DAY TO HAVE A GOOD DAY

I wasn't having the best day in the world. Truth be told, it felt like I hadn't had a fully good day in weeks—maybe even months. But during the drive home from a meeting, a conversation with my dad altered my perspective and changed my outlook moving forward.

Most statewide meetings for commodity groups and agriculture organizations take place in one of three places: Jefferson City, Columbia, or the Lake of the Ozarks. Making the trip across the state on Interstate 70, I used the time to call home and catch up with Beth—and then I typically called Mom and Dad to touch base. On one trip home from a mid-Missouri meeting, the conversation with Dad included me sharing frustrations from work. These included reductions in compensation, staffing cuts, and a recent meeting where management told my coworkers and me that our job was to "just shut up and learn." The frustration wasn't exclusive to me; conversations at work were mostly negative, and morale among employees was at an all-time low.

After listening to my rant, Dad's feedback was simple and to the point:

"I always figure when you get up in the morning, you have two choices when your feet hit the floor—you're either going to have a good day or a bad day. It's your choice as to how the day goes."

His words hit home and resonated with me.

I distinctly remember the next morning. As I walked down the sidewalk and stairs to get to the truck, the morning chill woke me up, and I told myself that, no matter what, I was going to have a good day. Within a few minutes of walking through the door at work, something went awry, and I had to remind myself I was still going to have a good day. Before long, conversations in the studio turned negative, so I knew it was best to walk away and focus on what was going right that day.

My goal was to conscientiously make the choice to have a good day for ten days in a row. Admittedly, there were moments of doubt. A few days in, after a particularly tough meeting, I caught myself falling into old habits. But I stopped, took a breath, and decided to refocus on what I could control. Each morning, as I stepped into the fresh morning air—feeling the familiar weight of my work bag and the crunch of gravel underfoot—I would pause, smile to myself, and repeat his words:

"Today's a good day to have a good day."

Plenty of Dad's advice still echoes in my mind—especially the most important piece: *every morning, when your feet hit the floor, pause for a moment and remember: it's a good day to be alive.* Set a goal to bring a smile to someone's face, stay positive, and make it a good day.

Richard Brand, my dad.
He gave me his best advice on an
ordinary day—and I've carried it
with me ever since.

ODE TO THE FFA ADVISOR

From 1928 to 1998, the streets of downtown Kansas City were overrun each fall with blue corduroy jackets, as the National FFA Convention brought members from across the country together to celebrate agricultural education, leadership, and career success.

Our FFA chapter advisor placed so much importance on attending the convention that he made a point to bring Greenhand members for a day. Olympic gymnast Bart Conner performed and spoke, we heard from a national officer, and we toured the career show. The experience was impactful and sparked the appetite of every student who attended. And the one who consistently fed that appetite for FFA? He stood at the front of the classroom—coaching contest teams, visiting members' farms, driving the bus to the next event, and prepping materials so each chapter member had the opportunity to do their best.

This is my ode to the FFA advisor.

Here's to the FFA advisor—the person who changes hats more times in a day than most people change their minds. They're a teacher, mentor, coach, bus driver, welder, speaker, accountant, and sometimes even a counselor. Their impact in the classroom reaches far beyond ag science, the greenhouse, or the machine shop. They model the very leadership they encourage in students—building confidence, teaching lifelong skills, and finding a way to make it fun.

These advisors guide students through complex projects, prepare them for contests, offer career advice, and push them to stretch beyond their comfort zones.

At every FFA meeting, the advisor takes their place beside the emblem of the owl. Their part of the opening ceremony goes like this:

"The owl is a time-honored emblem of knowledge and wisdom. Being older than the rest of you, I am asked to advise you from time to time as the need arises. I hope my advice will always be based on true knowledge and ripened with wisdom."

FFA advisors start their days before the first bell rings and end them long after the final one. They set up meeting spaces, run copies of contest prep materials, recruit local farmers for livestock judging, and ask fellow teachers to help coach students on oral reasons or speech skills. And their to-do list? It's filled with things no official job description ever includes.

They push students to be better while providing the safety net when things don't go as planned.

There's no one-size-fits-all. These advisors invest in students individually, tailoring encouragement and challenge based on each member's goals. Their reward is often a handshake, a high five, or maybe—on a really good day—a thank-you hug.

When I think back on my time in FFA, I think of my advisor, Dick Baldwin. His investment left a lasting mark on both my personal and professional life. From that first trip to the National FFA Convention, he saw potential in me I hadn't recognized in myself. Whether he was helping me perfect a speech, coaching our contest team, training racing pigs, or simply offering a word of encouragement, Mr. Baldwin's dedication shaped the future for so many of us.

It's easy to take for granted the time and effort these advisors put in. But the truth is, their work creates a ripple effect—impacting generations. Mr. Baldwin wasn't just a teacher. He was a mentor who challenged me to aim higher, think deeper, and never settle for less than my best. For that—and for so much more—I am forever grateful.

So here's to the FFA advisors like Mr. Baldwin, whose wisdom, encouragement, and unwavering belief in their students make all the difference. Their dedication to shaping future leaders in agriculture—and in life—goes far beyond the classroom.

HE WAS ALWAYS TEACHING

Before Mr. Bishop was ever a friend, he was a force.

Fourth graders—still in elementary school in the neighboring community of Pickering—had already heard about Mr. Bishop. From older siblings, from glimpses at school events, and from the kind of half-true urban legends only middle schoolers can spin. His reputation arrived before he did.

He taught science to 5th through 8th graders at North Nodaway, and when you walked into his classroom, you knew the rules were different. Not bad-different. *Better*-different. The kind of different that made you sit up straighter, listen harder, and think twice before even thinking about passing a note.

Other teachers had you sit in neat little rows. Mr. Bishop grouped us at lab tables—clusters of five or six students perched on stools, pretending not to be nervous. His classroom felt less like a lecture hall and more like a launch pad, literally and figuratively.

We called him "Mr. B," and he let us. No fuss about full names or titles. Mr. Bishop—John, though we never dared call him that—had the presence to command respect without needing ceremony. He was strong—physically, sure—but even more so in character, expectations, and the quiet way he shaped you without you even realizing.

Some called him tough. I called him *serious*. And I mean that in the best way.

He had a knack for pushing you to your limits without crossing the line. If you weren't paying attention, he knew. If you passed a note, you got caught. Every time. And then you earned the honor of staying after class for a little one-on-one discussion about your new hobby—which, by the way, ended right there.

Despite the tough-love approach, he made learning fun. Not gimmicky-fun, but engaging, thoughtful, stay-on-your-toes kind of fun. Every Friday meant ten new vocabulary words—usually tied to that week's lesson. One week, it was the planets, in order, from the sun to Pluto. (Yes, Pluto. Back when it still had its dignity.) That's how we picked up words like photosynthesis, chlorophyll, stroma, and stomata—big words we somehow didn't realize we were learning.

He gave pop quizzes like they were public service announcements. But here's the twist: he wanted you to succeed. He made sure his notes were on the board—detailed, clear, and always fair game. The challenge wasn't surprise—it was whether you cared enough to show up prepared.

I cared. Especially by seventh grade, when I decided I was going to be only the third student ever to score a perfect 100% for the semester in his class. I nailed everything—until the final test, where I missed two questions. When Mr. B handed it back, he looked at me with that dry grin and said, "Tough luck, Tom." No pity, no drama. Just the truth. And I respected him even more for it.

But his classroom was only part of the story.

Every spring, he led the 4-H Rocketry Club—pure volunteer time, fueled by his own enthusiasm and a few dollars' worth of mail-order Estes kits. We'd meet after school around 4 p.m., and those 40 minutes between the bell and blastoff were golden. You could clean erasers, run down to Wilson Grocery for a candy bar or a can of pop, or hang around and talk about rockets, outdoors, or whatever strange science fact had caught his interest that week.

We started with balsa wood fins—tracing, cutting, sanding. Then came the painting, the gluing, the nose cones. Mr. B inspected every rocket like it was destined for NASA. He stored them carefully in his classroom, where they sat in silent formation, waiting for their turn.

But he wasn't just building rockets. He was teaching science—quietly, constantly, cleverly. He taught us about launch angles, solid-fuel propulsion, timing, and altitude tracking using a homemade protractor device he was suspiciously proud of. He explained how fins and patterns and weight distribution affected flight. We learned momentum, friction, gravity—without ever cracking a textbook.

And then we launched. Rockets streaked into the sky, parachutes opening (usually), cardboard tubes spiraling back down like mission logs. Some soared. Some spun out like confused squirrels. Either way, we learned something.

And all of it—*all of it*—was his time, his energy, and, looking back, his joy.

He worked the gate at football games, collecting admission with that same western-style hat on his head. In the colder months, it was felt. In spring, straw. Never cowboy, exactly. Always Mr. Bishop.

He sponsored the high school science club, mostly to help us sell candy bars to fund the annual canoe trip on the Current River. Two days. Forty miles. Sleeping in tents, paddling through a stretch of Missouri he seemed to know like his own backyard.

He could spot caves before anyone else. He knew where the cold springs were (you had to stick your hand in), and where to pull over for a swim if we were ahead of schedule. If we were behind? The swims got a little shorter. Either way, the trip was a master class in geology, current flow, river reading, and how to paddle without looking like a fool. *Always teaching.*

Even after we moved up to high school, we still saw Mr. B in the halls. And he kept showing up—for reunions, for card exchanges, for little reminders that he hadn't stopped caring just because we'd graduated. He was that rare kind of teacher whose impact didn't fade. It just kept echoing.

I remember once he was giving me and another student a ride home. The other kid was late, so we started off slow, planning to spot him on the way down Schoolhouse Hill. A block befor the funeral home, an older woman flagged us down. "I've struck a child," she said.

And sure enough, there he was—collapsed by the curb. He'd fainted. Nothing serious, thank goodness, but the line stuck. Years later, that kid and I ended up in college together, and whenever one of us was late, we'd lean in and say, deadpan: "I've struck a child."

Mr. B would've laughed.

Because that's the thing—he wasn't just a teacher. He was a craftsman. A rocket-launching, river-paddling, hat-wearing legend who didn't just instruct—he imprinted. And for those of us lucky enough to sit at his lab tables or float alongside him down a river, his voice still echoes. In the way we prepare. In the way we teach others. In the way we show up.

He was the kind of teacher whose voice just kept echoing.

We still exchange Christmas cards. His handwriting hasn't changed.

Mr. Bishop was always teaching. And we're still learning.

> "A teacher affects eternity;
> he can never tell where his influence stops."
> — HENRY ADAMS

WHO'S THE AUDIENCE?

The years after high school are some of life's most influential—whether through college, trade school, the military, or work. Stepping into a new identity beyond those 13 years of schooling opens minds to new opinions and opportunities.

During college, I worked in the basement of Whitten Hall, editing stories and conducting interviews for the University of Missouri's *News Bites* radio news service. The work broadened my horizons and deepened my knowledge.

KMFC radio in Centralia—just up the road from Columbia—gave me my first on-air broadcast job, spinning records and playing pre-recorded programs. One day, the station manager complimented my work but asked who I was talking to when I introduced a song or read the weather forecast. I knew the station's target demographic, but hadn't pinpointed a specific listener. His suggestion: put Beth's picture on the control room board and talk to her. I did—and suddenly, I wasn't just talking; I was visiting with the audience. Visualizing them was key to making a connection.

One of the best reminders I've had in recent years came during a trip Beth and I took to Philo, Illinois. Just a few miles outside Champaign, Philo proudly calls itself "The Center of the Universe"—a playful motto that matches the pride and humor of its residents. Rural Philo is home to Dr. Jim Evans, a former University of Illinois agriculture communications professor whose warm personality and passion for the field impressed me from my earliest college days. His wife, Marlene, is equally remarkable. Together, they've cultivated multiple varieties of popcorn on their farm, hand-harvesting, shelling, and running it through a cleaner and shiner. Their popcorn has won top honors at the Illinois State Fair. The Evanses are the kind of neighbors everyone dreams of—welcoming, warm, with a postcard-perfect country home.

I never had Dr. Evans as an instructor, but he was a quiet influence during college—the first professor I met from another school who treated me like one of his own students, without trying to recruit me away from Missouri. He genuinely cared about students pursuing agriculture communications. Dr. Evans didn't just teach how to communicate—he asked why you were communicating. That friendship began 35 years ago and continues to this day.

During an interview with him a few years back, Dr. Evans asked, "Who's the audience?" before I even began. It seemed like a simple question, but the more I thought about it, the more I realized its depth. Whether it's a radio broadcast, a news article, or even a conversation, identifying the audience changes everything. Communication isn't just about sharing information—it's about connection. It's about making people feel like you're speaking directly to them— whether you're spinning records, giving a presentation, talking with coworkers, or writing a column.

> "The success of your presentation will be judged not by the knowledge you send but by what the listener receives."
> — LILLY WALTERS

I can think of at least two times Dr. Jim Evans asked me, "Who's the audience?" But it wasn't until I read Mike Wilson's 2020 article in Farm Progress that I fully understood the power of that question. (Mike now serves as Senior Executive Editor for Farm Progress.) He opened his piece by describing Jim asking him the same thing—a question that has quietly shaped the voice of nearly every agricultural publication today. Jim didn't just teach communication; he lived it, directing his answers to whoever needed to hear them.

That lesson still lives on. Every fall at the National FFA Convention, I work with broadcast interns—some who arrive with plenty of experience, and some who are just learning which end of the recorder to hold. Every student is different. But the starting point is always the same: ask, "Who's the audience?" The best lessons never stop teaching.

YOU STILL HAVE TO SMILE

The first semester of college didn't go the way I planned.

I started out as an ag engineering major, which sounded noble and useful on paper—but in practice, it wasn't clicking. I didn't love it, I wasn't thriving, and I wasn't exactly blowing the doors off academically. Eventually, I had a conversation with my Ag 101 instructor, Dr. Jan Dauve, who asked me a simple question: "What do you like doing?"

When I told him I liked to speak and write, he made a call that changed my life. He picked up the phone and dialed a guy named Joe Marks—a university professor and news director for agricultural research and extension.

A short while later, I took a walk from the Agriculture Building on Hitt Street to Whitten Hall on the edge of white campus. That was the first time I met Joe in person.

Upbeat, sharp, easy to talk to—Joe had the kind of energy that pulled you in. When he heard about my background—farm kid, FFA, public speaking—he suggested something I hadn't really considered: farm broadcasting. He talked about how important it was, how storytelling could make agriculture accessible, and how rural communities depended on voices they trusted. Joe had been an intern once too—in Wisconsin, working with a young broadcaster named Orion Samuelson, long before Orion became a legend at WGN in Chicago.

That conversation led to an internship with News Bites, a university radio service that fed ag stories and audio clips to stations across the Midwest. Joe got me set up, introduced me to broadcaster Jim Coyle at KRES in Moberly, and even encouraged me to apply to the newsroom at the National FFA Convention in Kansas City.

That convention—just one week—ended up being a launching pad. It connected me to a national network of ag broadcasters and led to my first trip to the farm broadcasters convention. If you want to trace where my career in farm broadcasting began, it wasn't at a podium or in a booth—it was with a phone call, a walk across campus, and a conversation with Joe Marks.

But he wasn't just a guy who opened doors. He stuck around.

Joe ended up being my advisor. When he took a sabbatical to Australia, he still stayed in touch with the department—and checked in on me from halfway around the world. Later, when I was working full-time as a broadcaster, he invited me back every fall to speak to his Intro to Ag Journalism class and broadcast my midday farm report live from campus. I'd share what a typical day looked like, offer some hard-earned lessons, and then we'd go grab lunch like old friends.

Every time I was back on campus, I made it a point to stop by and see him. His office in Whitten Hall became a kind of home base—a place where I'd set up for remote broadcasts, sure, but also where I'd sit down and catch up with someone who just got me.

Joe wasn't just a professor. He was a mentor, a cheerleader, and one of the best encouragers I've ever known. He smiled like it was his default setting. He ran marathons, always with that grin. When injuries finally took him off the running trails, he took up cycling—and did that with the same goofy joy that made him such a great coach to students.

There's one quote I'll never forget. He told me to take an acting class—something I didn't think I needed. I explained that I'd been in high school plays and didn't really see the point. He said: *"One morning, you'll wake up, stub your toe getting out of bed, trip on your way out the door, and the day will just get worse from there. But you'll still have to turn on a microphone and let your listeners know it's a great day. That class will help you do that."*

He was right. Joe usually was. On some of those days when life was messy or distracting, I specifically remember flipping on the mic and hearing his advice in my head.

Joe had planned to retire at the end of the school year in the spring. He was 61. Just after the New Year in 1999, I was back at work when I got a phone call from a student I knew. He told me Joe had been putting away Christmas decorations in the crawl space above his garage and fell—breaking some ribs. I smiled when I heard it. Not because he was hurt, but because I could picture him, smiling through the pain, cracking a joke with the ER nurse about the hazards of holiday cleanup.

But then the caller kept talking.

At the hospital, during a walk, one of the broken ribs had severed an artery. It hadn't shown up on the x-rays. He was gone in seconds.

I don't remember our last conversation. I wish I did. I'm sure it was full of his usual warmth, encouragement, and a joke or two—never knowing it would be the last one.

Joe Marks believed in broadcasting. But more than that, he believed in people. He believed in giving them the tools to find their voice—and the confidence to use it.

I wouldn't be where I am today without him.

And I wouldn't be the same kind of broadcaster without his encouragement, support, and teaching either.

"One of the greatest values of mentors is the ability to see ahead what others cannot see and to help them navigate a course to their destination."
— JOHN C. MAXWELL

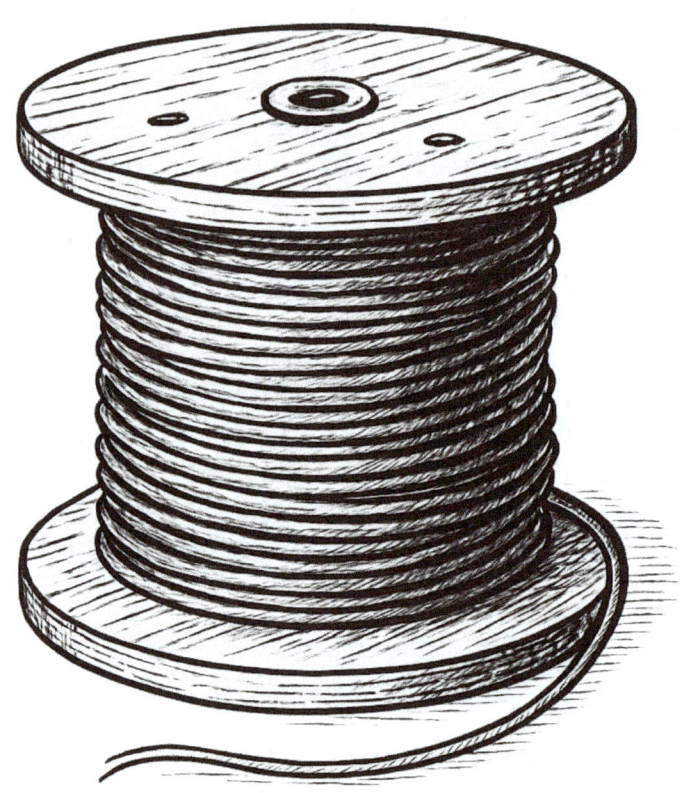

A LITTLE EXTRA...JUST IN CASE

Mutti Hardware in Hopkins was something special—
a world of possibilities surrounded you.

Entering from the south, the layout unfolded like a
treasure map.

On the left: fishing poles, tackle, BB guns, and ammunition.

Homewares were scattered throughout the central floor,
while the north side featured colorful paint displays
and the rhythmic hum of the paint mixer.

A small ramp led to an adjacent space filled with large
appliances—

washers, dryers, stoves, and ranges standing like sentries.

To the right of the entrance: tools and hardware,

anchored by the front counter where advice was given
and purchases finalized.

In the back, if you were lucky enough to venture there,
you'd find a workshop stocked with rope, wire, chain,
and a sturdy bench for repair work.

The space carried its own blend of odors:
varnish, hemp rope, oil on bolts and screws,
the occasional whiff of fresh paint,
and years of honest dust—

tracked in by boots, stirred by breeze through the
open door.

But under it all lingered the unmistakable scent
of tobacco—

from Bill Melvin's pipe. I never knew the brand,
but I'm convinced the blend included cherry.

That faint aroma was as much a part of the store
as the goods on the shelves,
a scent that carried the very essence of the community.

George Mutti was the steady heart of the front counter—
a presence as dependable as the store itself.

He didn't just help you find what you needed.
He asked how you were doing.
And he *listened*.

His depth of knowledge matched the store's inventory.
You didn't just leave with supplies.
You left with confidence—and maybe a story.
One trip stands out:
I was there to buy bell wire for a train layout.
"How many feet?" George asked.
I didn't know.
So we figured it out together.
In the back, we unrolled the wire across a marked
stretch of floor.
George watched quietly.
Before cutting, he pulled a little extra and said,
"Just in case."
These days, few places still sell wire by the foot.
Big box stores offer only spools—25, 50, 100 feet.
Even if you only need 30, you'll have to buy 50.
That kind of care—of measured, thoughtful service—
feels like a relic.
Mutti Hardware wasn't just a store.
It was a cornerstone.
And George Mutti wasn't just a shopkeeper.
He was a craftsman of people.
George was the extra you didn't know you needed.

"Nearly every moment
of every day,
we have the opportunity
to give something to someone else—
our time, our love, our resources."
— S. TRUETT CATHY

A GOOD IMPRESSION

On the east side of the street in downtown Hopkins, tucked between the bar and Ferrellgas, was a little shop called Cross Printing. It sat just up the street from Mutti Hardware and diagonally across from Motsinger Insurance. The kind of place you might pass by without thinking twice—unless you were a dusty, sweaty kid on a bike, pocket full of change, and a deep appreciation for paper.

Russell and Anna Cross ran the place. They were soft-spoken and professional, polite in that warm, small-town way that made you feel important even when you weren't. And let's be honest—I was not. I was a kid. A farm kid who biked the 2½ miles into town to make the rounds. I'd check out the new stamps at the Post Office. Grab a pop at Wilson's Grocery. Try to catch Maurice Peve at the feed store. Then swing by Mutti Hardware to smell the rope and varnish—or maybe buy BBs But my last stop was almost always Cross Printing.

The place smelled exactly like it should—ink-forward, with backnotes of oiled machinery and something warm and metallic that I later learned came from the old lead type-setting equipment. It was a scent you didn't forget, especially if you loved words, paper, and machines that made both come alive.

Anna worked the front counter. She had a gentle way of answering my endless questions, even when my "purchase" was just a few sheets of paper for making airplanes or drawing pigs that looked suspiciously like cows. She never rushed me. If she was busy, I didn't notice. She'd show me the different weights and colors, ask what I was planning to use the paper for, and offer advice like I was her biggest client—not just a 10-year-old with pocket change and a sticky bottle cap in my pocket.

Russell would occasionally invite me into the back to see the press. The clink of type, the hum of the machines, the drawers of neatly arranged letters—it all felt like some secret world. A world where you could say something loud without raising your voice, just by pressing it into paper. They printed auction bills, newsletters (including *The Hopkins Journal* at one time), business cards, and what I considered to be the pinnacle of signage: a heavy card-stock warning that read, **NO TRESPASSING: Survivors Will Be Prosecuted.**

Now that was a sign.

Naturally, I bought one for my bedroom door. Nothing deters siblings like a casual threat of legal action.

Sure, we'd done 4-H field trips to Cross Printing, but the best visits were the solo missions—when it felt like I was getting a behind-the-scenes pass just for being curious. And that curiosity was always welcomed. It wasn't just tolerated. It was encouraged. That kind of personalized attention doesn't come with a price tag, but I paid anyway.

Once I'd secured my precious sheets of paper, I'd bike home—usually against the wind, gripping my treasure tightly and trying not to crinkle the corners. I never carried the paper around town. I learned early that if you do, it flaps, folds, or flies. Cross Printing was always the final stop before heading back to the gravel road and the farm.

Today, that very building is the Hopkins Historical Society Museum. Which feels right. Because it was always more than a print shop. It was a place where stories began—some pressed into paper, others pedaled home in a sweaty kid's backpack.

> "Sometimes the smallest things
> take up the most room
> in your heart."
> — A. A. MILNE

I had no idea when I walked into that little shop I'd carry the smell of ink and kindness with me for the rest of my life.

ADVICE TO MY GRANDSONS FOR SCOOPING SNOW

When our grandsons, Micah and Shiloh, had just turned six and four, it made my day when I received a text message with a photo of them outside in the snow, beaming as they held shovels in their hands. They enjoy being outdoors and have reached the age where they're independent enough to spend time playing in the snow with limited supervision. From that age, I knew it wouldn't be long until they were ready to take on the entire job of clearing snow from the walks and driveway. They're both eager helpers—pushing snow with the optimism that it's making a bigger pile to dive into later.

Unless they migrate far enough south to escape winter entirely, a lifetime of snow removal awaits them. So, in the spirit of preparation, here's my advice:

Start with the sidewalk. It may seem like a small detail, but every step compacts the snow, making it harder to clear when you're cold and tired. If your vehicle isn't in the garage, clear it off next—then scoop the snow away from it. That way, the next time it snows, you'll come back to a clean spot instead of a packed-down mess that freezes harder with every storm.

Plan your path. Whether using a scoop or a snowblower, think before you throw. With a lighter snow, you can fling it far. But with a heavy, wet one? You want to touch it once. Consider carving a center path first, then working from the middle outward. And when you clear the edges, throw the snow far—you may not see bare ground again for months.

Remember the mailman. They're out six days a week, no matter the weather. A clear path across the yard or up to the porch is a gift. And while fires aren't what we usually worry about in winter, keeping the hydrant dug out is a small kindness that might save someone's home—or life—as it saves precious minutes.

Help your neighbor. Whether it's a widow next door or a couple up the street, surprise them by clearing their walk. If they try to pay you, decline. Remind them of the good they've done for others. That's how real community works.

Clean up after. Clear off your shovel so it doesn't leave puddles in the garage. Do the same with the snowblower if you used it. Hang your bibs or coveralls by the belt loop instead of the elastic straps so they dry properly and keep the braces from stretching. Tuck your bootlaces inside so they're dry the next morning. If you don't have a boot mat, a few folded newspapers work fine.

I imagine there are plenty of snow-filled days ahead for Micah and Shiloh—days of scooping, building forts, and discovering that clearing the walk is just as important as clearing the driveway. And with any luck, they'll learn that small efforts—done well and done kindly—leave the biggest impressions. Especially when there's a mug of cocoa waiting at the end of it all.

Micah and Shiloh—shovel-ready,
and always up for an adventure.

WHAT IT COST, WHAT IT GAVE

Freedom doesn't just arrive with a sparkler and a grill—it's paid for in sweat, sacrifice, and sometimes, the silence of a name no longer known. This final section reflects on what it means to live in a place where fireworks fly and parades march—only because someone else stood watch.

These stories aren't sad—but they are sacred. They remind us why we celebrate Independence Day, *not "the Fourth," and why silence at Arlington still speaks louder than words.*

"Those who have long enjoyed such privileges as we enjoy forget in time that men have died to win them."
— FRANKLIN D. ROOSEVELT

FIRST TIME IN D.C.

In 1994, I was still learning the ropes of farm broadcasting. I had some experience as a DJ and had edited stories for University Extension, so I wasn't new to radio. But joining the Brownfield Ag Network in Jefferson City was a whole new ballgame—especially when it came to policy.

I'd been on the job since August and was slowly finding my footing. My daily responsibilities included broadcasting market reports and ag news updates, and I quickly realized I had a lot to learn about legislative coverage. Thankfully, the team at Brownfield was supportive and patient, giving me opportunities to attend meetings, talk with ag leaders, and get a better grasp of how policy stories came together.

That's when I got the chance to attend the National Association of Farm Broadcasting's Washington Watch— my first trip to the nation's capital.

It didn't feel like just another event. It felt like stepping onto a bigger stage.

In D.C., I sat at tables with commodity group leaders and national policymakers. I had the chance to ask questions of the Secretary of Agriculture. I met with lawmakers from both chambers of Congress and introduced myself to the communications staff in the offices we regularly covered—people I'd only known over the phone.

Two moments still stand out.

One was an interview with Senator Richard Lugar of Indiana, conducted in the stairwell of one of the Senate office buildings. The other was with Senator Bob Kerrey of Nebraska, who asked, "Mind if we walk and talk?" I said yes, of course—and suddenly found myself wandering the back halls of the Capitol, microphone in hand, trying to keep pace. We wrapped the interview in front of a short, unmarked door. Senator Kerrey shook my hand, ducked through it, and stepped directly onto the Senate floor. I stood there for a second, slightly stunned, then turned and tried to remember how to get out.

That first trip to Washington taught me more than any classroom could. And it sparked a connection that's lasted three decades.

Since then, I've been back to D.C. more than 50 times. I've come to know the rhythm of its streets and the weight of its memorials. Some trips were quick. Others changed me. Each time, I carried something new home—another piece of what it means to be part of a nation built on decisions, sacrifice, and ideals worth understanding.

My first trip to D.C. was also my first experience with the Metro system—and with how confusing city navigation can be when you're from the Midwest.

Fresh off the plane at Reagan National, I figured I'd try public transit. The hotel was just a block from the Metro station. Easy, right?

A Metro attendant gave me directions. I boarded the train with my bag of broadcast gear and a suitcase with no wheels (rookie mistake) and followed his instructions to the letter.

Unfortunately, the letter didn't include which quadrant of D.C. I was supposed to be in.

Washington, as I soon learned, is divided into four zones— NW, NE, SE, and SW. I exited in the wrong one. Very wrong. Let's just say the scenery didn't match the hotel brochure.

Several blocks, two postal workers, and one warming barrel later, I retraced my steps, made it back underground, and found the right station.

It was my first lesson in D.C. geography—and a reminder that not all "one-block walks" are created equal.

THE TOMB GUARD

What is the cost of freedom?

It's a question we ask—sometimes quietly, sometimes aloud—on a weekend filled with flags, flowers, and parades. It's a question that sits beneath every headstone at Arlington and every cemetery that holds a soldier's grave. And sometimes, the answer doesn't come in words.

Sometimes it walks in silence.

I had the honor of visiting Arlington National Cemetery and interviewing a man named Jon Brisiel—a soldier with the 3rd U.S. Infantry Regiment, known as The Old Guard. He was a Tomb Guard at the Tomb of the Unknown Soldier.

You've seen the ceremony, maybe in person or on video—the *changing of the guard*, carried out with military precision every thirty minutes. But until you've heard what it takes to be that guard, you might not fully understand the weight they carry.

Jon told me their standard is simple: perfection. Not excellence. Not "close enough." *Perfection.*

Only about one in four who try out make it through. Even then, they aren't immediately accepted. For the first two weeks, it's called *"temporary duty."* You're not even assigned to the platoon. You're being watch and evaluated. The first test includes a physical training exam, memorizing the first seven of seventeen pages of tomb guard knowledge, mastering the changing of the guard sequence, and learning how to alter and maintain every single detail of your uniform.

You don't pass unless it's *perfect.*

Final uniform inspections allow for a variance of no more than 1/32 of an inch. Measurements are made down to 1/64th. You train to walk with exact rhythm and pace— counting numbers in your head, guided by a metronome until that walk becomes second nature. Jon told me: *"What people see is a soldier walking.* What they don't realize is it takes six months to a year to walk like that."

And all of it—every step, every adjustment, every second of silence—is for those who cannot speak for themselves. The

Unknown Soldiers. The ones who gave everything. Not just their lives. Their names. Their identities.

Jon didn't talk much about his role. Not because he wasn't proud, but because he didn't want any praise directed his way. "We don't do it for all the onlookers," he told me. "That ceremony is executed with military precision—not for the crowd, but for the heroes who gave not only their lives, but their identities"

Only 700 soldiers have ever earned the Army's rarest badge: the Tomb Guard Identification Badge. And yet every man or woman who wears that badge knows: they are not the heroes. They're the caretakers of sacrifice.

Working guard duty doesn't just wear on the soldier— it wears out the uniform. After each shift, the guards return and begin again, restoring every crease, polishing every detail. As Jon put it, "While you're guarding, you're destroying your uniform. And as soon as your shift ends, you're already working to make sure it still looks perfect."

It's humbling, he said, to see the crowds react—to feel the silence settle over them. But the honor isn't in being watched. It's in who they are watching over.

Memorial Day is *not* just about *remembrance*—it's about reflection. It's about confronting, however briefly, the true cost of freedom. And standing at the Tomb of the Unknown Soldier, you realize something: *silence has a sound*. It echoes off white marble and the shoulders of those who carry the memory forward with every perfectly measured step.

So when you see the flags, the parades, the wreaths— pause. Not just out of tradition, but out of recognition. *Some gave everything. Some gave even their names.*

Today, and every hour since March 25, 1926, a guard still walks.

Not for recognition. Not for cameras.

But for silence.

For sacrifice.

For freedom.

A BOY NAMED JOE

When my dad was drafted into the Army in 1952 for the Korean War, he knew exactly what that meant.

His father had served in World War I.

His brother, Robert, served in World War II.

He'd seen the men who came home different—and heard the names of those who didn't come home at all. So when the letter arrived, he didn't hesitate. He packed his things and reported, carrying with him the quiet weight of knowing what was at stake.

He always said the Army was one of the best things that ever happened to him. "Straightened me up," he'd say. It was a good experience in discipline. The Army suited him, and he worked hard. He was promoted from enlisted to Private, made the rank of Corporal just three days later, and eventually earned the rank of Sergeant.

He had originally been assigned to serve on the front lines, fighting along the 38th parallel. But early on, he got a taste of fate. At an assembly of his unit, a commanding officer asked if anyone knew how to drive a truck. Dad raised his hand. That single moment pulled him off the front lines and into supply duty—where he served just south of the 38th, hauling ammunition, issuing gear, and keeping the logistics running through the freezing Korean winter.

We heard lots of stories about his time in the Army— basic training, his friend Goodyear, his commanding officer Colonel Kermit Bell, even running into Hopkins native Rube Turner while overseas. Dad once gave up a weekend pass to Japan because he was needed at the base. That plane went down in flight. Everyone onboard was killed. He carried that with him the rest of his life.

However, the story he told most wasn't about ranks or regulations.

It was about a little boy who needed a home.

One night, while serving as Sergeant of the Guard, Dad was making rounds with Goodyear when he suddenly stopped.

"Did you hear that?"

"Hear what?"

"A pig cough."

Goodyear chuckled. "You're dreaming about the farm again." But Dad knew what he'd heard. He shined his flashlight toward a pile of brush and broken debris. And there, curled beneath a coat and little else, was a young Korean boy.

The boy had been in that brush pile for days. As they later pieced together, he and his family had been swept up in one of the "pushes" from North Korean forces—civilians driven south with nowhere to go. His English was minimal, but when Dad asked how long he'd been there, the boy answered with this:

"First day—hungry.

Next day—more hungry.

Third day—no hungry anymore."

He didn't say it with drama. Just fact. The kind that settles into your bones.

Dad brought him into the supply tent, which until then he'd had all to himself. He got him clean clothes, a hot meal, and a safe place to sleep. The plan was simple: the chaplain would be visiting in a few days and could take the boy to an orphanage the unit supported financially.

But the chaplain never made it. His jeep broke down. The visit was delayed. And in the meantime... the little boy became one of them. They called him Joe.

Dad had a uniform altered to fit him. Joe helped out around the base. He played checkers with the General at the neighboring Air Force base. He became, as Dad once put it, "the kid brother I never had."

By the time the chaplain showed up weeks later, it was too late. Nobody was sending Joe to the orphanage.

Dad never stopped smiling when he told the story. He'd shake his head at Joe's cleverness. Laugh at the checkers story. Pause when he talked about how attached they'd all become. That boy had crawled into a brush pile to hide — and somehow climbed into all their hearts instead.

When Dad's tour ended, he seriously considered bringing Joe home to Hopkins. But one of his superiors, Colonel Feeney, sat him down for a talk.

"Are there any Korean kids in your hometown?"

"No, sir."

"What about in the nearest city?"

"No, sir."

"Then you know what kind of life he'd have. You'd love him. But the world might not."

That truth hit hard. Dad knew what was right — and what was real.

When he shipped out at the end of his service, Joe stayed. Later, he learned Colonel Feeney had taken Joe with him to Japan — set him up with school, kept him close. Dad never saw him again.

From time to time, he'd talk about tracking Joe down. But this was a different era. No internet. No search tools. Just hope.

What he had — what he kept — was memory. A few photographs. A story that lit up his face every time he told it.

Some boys become family, even if you only get to borrow them for a while.

And some moments stay with a man for the rest of his life.

A boy named Joe was one of them.

Sergeant Rittenhouse, Joe,
and my dad, Richard Brand

JUST OFF THE BEATEN PATH

Washington, D.C. holds a special place in my heart. Over the past three decades, I've visited the capital more than 50 times. Each trip has offered another chance to walk the wide paths of history and feel the weight of sacrifice carved into stone and bronze.

One of the most meaningful parts of my time in D.C. has been leading a leadership training program that includes a walking tour of the National Mall. It's not a casual stroll. It's a journey—one that begins between the towering Washington Monument and the World War II Memorial, with the Lincoln Memorial just visible in the distance.

Right there at the start, a plaque connects the dots between sacrifice and service. It links the enduring legacies of George Washington and Abraham Lincoln to the stories remembered in these memorials. It sets the tone. You're not just sightseeing—you're stepping into memory.

From there, we move toward the Vietnam Veterans Memorial. The names are the first thing you notice—more than 58,000 of them—cut into the black granite wall with a quiet dignity that commands your attention. I try to help the next generation connect with those names. One story I share is about three boys from a small Utah town, raised within three blocks of one another, who all died within days of each other in Vietnam. It's personal, and it's powerful.

Next, we stand at the foot of Lincoln—his statue larger than life, his words engraved into the stone: the Gettysburg Address to one side, his Second Inaugural on the other. From there, it's on to the Korean War Memorial, where 19 steel soldiers move through a ghostly field, reflected in a black wall etched with the faces of those who served. I pause here to tell the story of a young man who volunteered for a job. He didn't know it at the time, but it would change his life forever.

Then we continue to the Martin Luther King Jr. Memorial—carved from the mountain of despair, standing tall as the stone of hope—and on to the Franklin Delano Roosevelt Memorial, where waterfalls, quotes, and bronze sculptures stretch across blocks, telling the story of a presidency that guided the country through some of its darkest days.

But my favorite stop? It's not the biggest. It's not the most visited. It's tucked across the street from the main path, quiet and easy to miss. It's the George Mason Memorial.

George Mason doesn't get a lot of headlines. But he had a hand in nearly every part of the founding. A mentor to George Washington, and called the wisest man of his generation by Thomas Jefferson, Mason was a champion for individual rights and a driving force behind the Bill of Rights.

His memorial is modest—almost humble. But maybe that's what makes it matter more. It reminds us that leadership doesn't always come with trumpets and spotlight. Sometimes it lives in the footnotes. Sometimes it sits just off the beaten path.

COLONEL BELL

Though I only met Colonel Kermit Bell once, his story had been part of our family's memory for decades. He served as my father's commanding officer during the Korean War, a man my dad spoke of with unmistakable respect. When I finally had the chance to hear the Colonel's story firsthand, I realized his life wasn't just remarkable—it was a quiet echo of service, humility, and purpose that deserved to be remembered.

Kermit Bell never set out to make a career in the military. But by the time he retired from the Army, he had served in three wars, worn the uniform for over two decades, and left a legacy that stretched from the muddy riverbanks of Illinois to the helicopter pads of Vietnam.

He grew up on a farm near Batchtown, Illinois. In 1945, as World War II was drawing to a close, Bell voluntarily enlisted in the regular Army. He beat the draft to have more control over his service—but also, as he later admitted, to secure the G.I. Bill. That three-year guarantee was the only way he saw college as a possibility. Even as a teenager, Bell was quietly strategic.

At first, he worked as an aviation engineer and briefly considered truck-driving school. But a superior officer saw something more and chastised him for thinking too small. Bell took the advice to heart. He applied to West Point.

At the time, the Army allowed 40 enlisted men per year to be selected for the academy. Bell was one of them. He went through prep school, earned his spot, and began a new chapter among the country's military elite.

"It was a great time to be at West Point," Bell said later. "We had all the heroes of World War II teaching."

He graduated in 1952. Among his classmates were future astronauts and Medal of Honor recipients. There was Ed White, who died tragically in the Apollo 1 fire, and Mike Collins, who kept vigil in lunar orbit while Armstrong and

Aldrin walked the surface below. Bell belonged to a class that shaped history. But he, too, was already on his way.

Not long after graduation, he was sent to Korea.

There, Bell was assigned to the 30th Artillery Battalion, stationed on Korea's west coast. Initially in charge of a gun battery, he later transitioned to the Headquarters Battery, managing the administrative backbone of the battalion. Though Korea was defined by hardship and tension, one of Bell's most enduring memories wasn't of a battle—but of a boy.

"One morning my soldiers found a young Korean boy laying outside the tent, half froze to death," Bell said. "They brought him inside, put him in a bunk, and covered him with blankets. I think it took him about a week to thaw out. I guess we named him Joe."

It was the unit's supply sergeant—Sergeant Brand— who took charge of caring for Joe. The soldiers made the boy part of their family, ensuring his safety, teaching him, feeding him. By the end of Bell's tour, Joe had become so attached to the battalion that higher command took an interest in his future. When the unit left, Joe was placed in the care of a colonel at headquarters who made sure the boy remained safe.

"I tell you," Bell said, "when you get a bunch of soldiers around and somebody's in need, they're going to find a way to take care of them."

Korea wasn't supposed to be his future. When Bell first enlisted, he imagined three years, maybe four. But war has a way of extending timelines, and duty has a way of convincing people to stay. He remained in the military. And then came Vietnam.

By 1967, Bell had become a base commander—a role he compared to being the mayor of a small town. His base stretched about two square miles, a runway running down the center. Helicopters were constantly arriving and departing, and despite being in command, Bell had been quietly teaching himself to fly.

Then one night, the base ran short on pilots.

Bell, underqualified but undeterred, took the controls himself and flew the mission. The objective was completed. The helicopter, however, returned with more dents than it left with.

"That particular incident... the first Division command didn't want to recognize the fact that I had done that," Bell recalled, grinning. "So they had the Vietnamese government give me a medal for it. They had the choice of giving me a medal or giving me a court-martial."

By the end of his Vietnam tour, Bell had earned five Bronze Stars.

When he returned to the United States in 1968, his next assignment came swiftly and seriously: Memphis, Tennessee, following the assassination of Dr. Martin Luther King Jr. Bell was placed in charge of coordinating civil affairs in the event of riots or unrest. For two years, he worked to ensure military preparedness and civilian cooperation during one of the most charged periods in the country's modern history.

He retired from the military as a lieutenant colonel. But he still wasn't finished.

In his forties, Bell went back to school. He studied to become an optometrist—this time surrounded by classmates the age of his children. They teased him relentlessly for being "the old man," but Bell held his own and earned his degree. He started his second career, treating patients and running his own practice in the same quiet, steadfast manner he'd brought to every base, battalion, and bunker.

He built a home in Batchtown himself—an octagon-shaped, dome-style structure that reflected both his curiosity and craftsmanship. At the top, he constructed a crow's nest with a sweeping view of the Mississippi River bottom. From there, you could see the water wind its way through the Illinois countryside—a fitting perch for a man whose life had crossed oceans, conflicts, and decades of history.

Colonel Kermit Bell passed away in 2024. His story, though, still echoes: in the soldiers he served with, the classmates he outpaced, the boy he helped save, the lives he improved, and the quiet example he left behind.

When I called him to let him know Dad had passed, Colonel Bell's response was quiet and sure:

"He was a good soldier."

The right words, at the right time.

He followed the call with a handwritten note to the family. A final act of respect from a man who understood the weight of service—and never failed to honor it.

He thought he'd serve three years.

He gave more than twenty.

And never once did he stop showing up.

Kermit Bell — U.S. Military Academy, Class of 1952

"The soldier is the Army.
No army is better than its soldiers.
The Soldier is also a citizen.
In fact, the highest obligation and privilege of citizenship
is that of bearing arms for one's country."
— GEORGE S. PATTON

HISTORY BENEATH HIS FEET

An architect or carpenter knows a place because they helped build it. Others know places like they belong to them. That was Tom Sherlock. His connection to Arlington National Cemetery may be the strongest of anyone in its history.

I met Tom on a visit to Arlington National Cemetery in 2010. At the time, I was gathering interviews for *The American Countryside*, and someone at the cemetery—knowing I was drawn to stories that mattered—suggested I talk with Tom.

It's still one of the most meaningful conversations I've ever had.

Sherlock started at Arlington in the mid-1970s, fresh out of the University of Maryland. He helped visitors look up grave locations and answer questions in the welcome center. When historical inquiries arrived by mail, he volunteered to answer them. Not because it was glamorous work, but because he wanted to get the facts right.

"There wasn't a historian on staff back then," he told me, "but there were a lot of stories that deserved to be remembered."

Eventually, the cemetery superintendent agreed—and made the title official: Arlington Cemetery Historian.

He described Arlington as unlike any other place a historian might serve. "Most historical jobs are focused on an era," he said. "Gettysburg has the Civil War. But this… this stretches from the Revolutionary War to today. We make history here every day."

And he wasn't exaggerating. His job included everything from arranging a visit for the Queen of England to helping oversee the burial—and eventual disinterment—of the Vietnam Unknown. But he always circled back to the same point: that it's the moments you don't expect that often stay with you.

"You see people at one of the worst times in their lives," he said. "Then maybe a year later, they come back and thank you—for something you don't even remember doing. Maybe it was a look, or a moment of silence. But it mattered. And at that time, for them, it meant everything."

He didn't say that for effect. He said it because it was true.

Tom walked me through parts of the cemetery most visitors never see. Yes, there were the places people expect—the Tomb of the Unknowns, Kennedy's grave, the changing of the guard. But then he took me to Section 27.

It sits quietly along the edge of the cemetery, without crowds or ceremony. It's the final resting place for nearly 3,800 formerly enslaved people—men, women, and children buried under headstones marked "citizen," or in many cases, just "unknown." Many were stacked, nameless, like cordwood, after disease and neglect swept through the freedman encampments during and after the Civil War. That section—its vastness, its loneliness—stuck with me.

So many of us walk through Arlington and see it as a place of polished stone and national memory. But Tom saw every inch of it—what lay beneath the manicured grass, and what so many had forgotten. He understood how many stories went untold. And he spent his career making sure they weren't forgotten.

There are over 400,000 graves at Arlington now. Most visitors will never know the names. But Tom did. Or at the very least, he wanted to.

The afternoon we spent together went too fast. But the impact stayed. It broadened my understanding of a sacred place—and deepened my appreciation for people like Tom Sherlock, who didn't just preserve history, but carried it with him, one name at a time.

THE LADIES WHO ALWAYS SHOW UP

They represent the quietest kind of honor.

Most people have never heard of the Arlington Ladies. That's not a criticism—just a fact. They don't seek attention. They don't wear rank. And they certainly don't expect applause. But on any weekday morning, in any kind of weather, you'll find one standing quietly at Arlington National Cemetery—there to do one thing: make sure no service member is buried alone.

I first learned about them while setting up interviews at Arlington National Cemetery. It was Thomas Sherlock, the cemetery's former historian, who suggested I connect with them. I had the chance to interview Margaret Mensch, chair of the Army's Arlington Ladies. She was calm, composed, and humble. But when she described what they do, there was no mistaking the weight of it.

"That's our most important job," she told me. "We're there when there's nobody."

And sometimes, there really is nobody. Just the Arlington Lady, a military escort, the chaplain, and a folded flag. In those cases, the Lady may even be the one to receive the flag on behalf of the family—if no family could attend.

Margaret said it happens more often than most would guess. Veterans who've outlived friends and family. Active-duty service members without next of kin. Even children. "You come away with tears in your eyes," she said. "Especially when there are little kids involved."

The Army has about 50 volunteers—many former military spouses, ranging in age from their 40s to their 80s. They serve on rotation, usually two on duty at a time, attending 8 to 10 funerals a day. They stand quietly, faithfully, and with grace and dignity.

I also interviewed representatives from the Air Force and Navy. Every woman I spoke to carried the same quiet reverence. They weren't mourners—they were witnesses. Sentinels. The human presence among uniforms and ceremony. One Navy Lady put it perfectly: "We don't cry. We're not there to grieve. We're there to honor."

But of course, the line isn't always that clear. A 10-year-old hugging your legs. A widow who clings to your arm. The burial of a young escort you once served alongside. These are not easy moments. But they show up anyway.

One of the Ladies said it best: "It doesn't matter if we're burying a four-star general or a private. Everyone deserves someone to say thank you at their grave."

And that's exactly what they do.

We live in a noisy world. But the Arlington Ladies are proof that dignity still matters. That quiet still matters. And that honor, when it's real, doesn't need to raise its voice.

Some people serve on the front lines. Others serve at the finish line. But all of them remind us that no one gets there alone. And thanks to the Arlington Ladies—no one leaves alone either.

INDEPENDENCE DAY

For nearly two and a half centuries, the United States of America has marked its independence from British rule. Even though the movement to do so had been brewing for quite some time, one has to wonder about the reaction of King George III when he first read those words of rebellion.

Technically, it was July 2 when the Second Continental Congress approved the resolution of independence, and the Declaration wasn't signed until early August. But July 4 became the date we celebrate, as that was the date shown on the publicized version of the Declaration of Independence.

Andy Rooney provided commentary on CBS' *60 Minutes* for 33 years. His insight and wit were always enjoyable—even when you might find yourself in disagreement with his philosophy. So, in my best Andy Rooney voice, I offer the following:

It's always seemed odd to me that so many people call this holiday the *Fourth of July*. I've never heard anyone refer to Christmas as celebrating *the twenty-fifth of December*. Mexico has their *Cinco de Mayo* holiday, but it's actually a celebration of a military victory; their Independence Day comes in mid-September. Most other countries celebrate an Independence or Constitution Day, but here in the United States, we've chosen to highlight the calendar square instead of the cause. Why focus on the day, rather than the declaration?

Could George Washington and the other Founding Fathers have known the ultimate cost of drawing this line in the sand? Surely not. Many would face hardships, torture, and even death. But I believe some of them did understand what it might cost—and it was their courage, and their hope for what was to come, that led them to risk everything.

George Washington had the vision, saying:

"Liberty, when it begins to take root, is a plant of rapid growth."

John Adams shared a similar vision for the new nation. In a letter to his wife, he wrote:

149

"I am apt to believe that it will be celebrated, by succeeding generations, as the great anniversary festival. It ought to be commemorated, as the Day of Deliverance by solemn Acts of Devotion to God Almighty. It ought to be solemnized with pomp and parade, games, sports, guns, bells, bonfires and illuminations from one end of this continent to the other from this time forward forever more."

He also added:

"I am well aware of the toll and blood and treasure that it will cost us to maintain this declaration, and support and defend these states. I can see that the end is more than worth all the means. And that posterity will triumph in the days of transaction."

Let's get back to the intention of the declaration and call this great day what it is: **Independence Day**—a reminder of that sacrifice and dedication of our Founding Fathers and those citizens who saw this as more than just the *Fourth of July.*

"We must be free
not because we claim freedom,
but because we practice it."
— WILLIAM FAULKNER

"Turns out, memory
isn't always gentle—
but it is always generous."

THE LAST WORD...FOR NOW

If you've made it this far, thank you.

These stories—fueled by gravel roads, pickup rides, front porch wisdom, and the occasional threatened welt—weren't written to impress. They were written to remember. To stitch together the moments that made a life. Some of them are muddy. Some are funny. A few still ache a little. But they all matter.

I'll admit, writing this has been more emotional than I expected. There were moments I laughed out loud retelling something to Beth, and a few where the tears caught me off guard. Turns out, memory isn't always gentle—but it is always generous. This has been one of the best trips down memory road I've ever taken. And I've taken a lot.

If this book reminded you of a place, a person, or a time you thought you'd forgotten... I'm glad. That means it worked. That means we took the ride together.

Of course, not all the stories fit here. Some are still rattling around in the toolbox. Others are waiting to be dug out like old fence staples or rolled up like twine for another season.

So stay tuned.

Because the next chapter's already got a title: *You Have to Leave If You Want to Come Back.*

And as a certain time-traveling scientist once said:

"Roads? Where we're going, we don't need roads."

ACKNOWLEDGEMENTS

To Beth, who hears every story before anyone else does—thank you for your patience, encouragement, edits, and the occasional eye-roll that made its way into the final version anyway.

To Kay Wilson at the *Nodaway News Leader*—thank you. Your invitation to publish that first feature in the paper is what officially started all of this, and I'm grateful for your confidence and kindness.

To my family—thank you for living the stories with me, telling them better than I ever could, and giving me a lifetime of moments to draw from. Mom and Dad, in particular, handed me a full library's worth of memories.

Mom, you once shared a poem:

There was a wise owl who lived in an oak.
The more he saw, the less he spoke.
The less he spoke, the more he heard.
Why can't we all be like that bird?

That one stuck with me. So did Dad saying "Listen!" instead of "Shut up"when he really wanted us to pay attention. That small difference in tone taught me a lot—not just about words, but how to use them.

To Andrew McCrea, Max Armstrong, and Mike Hergert—thank you for showing me what great storytelling looks like. I've had the good fortune to learn from you, work alongside you, and sit on the front row for some of the finest stories ever told.

To the readers who encouraged me over the years, and to the friends who kept asking, "When's the book coming out?"— thank you for giving me a reason to start it *and* finish it.

Select line art illustrations throughout this book were created with the help of AI and guided by the author's creative direction.

And if this is the end of one book...

I suppose that means another story is just getting started.

ABOUT THE AUTHOR

Tom Brand grew up outside Hopkins, Missouri, where gravel roads, farm fields, and family stories shaped a lifelong appreciation for faith, community, and hard work. He's a proud graduate of North Nodaway High School and attended the University of Missouri, where he studied agriculture communications and spent time connected to the tail of Truman the Tiger.

His career began behind a microphone, spending 19 years as a farm broadcaster for the Brownfield Network, KMA, and KFEQ radio. He covered everything from local livestock shows to international agriculture news in Mexico, Cuba, London, and Hong Kong — interviewing farmers, politicians, and the occasional celebrity like Jerry Clower, Danny Glover, Scott Hamilton, Henry Winkler, and Mike Rowe.

After serving as Executive Director for a national association supporting farm broadcasters — continuing his work to connect rural voices across the country — Tom shifted focus back to local impact as Director of the St. Joseph Community Alliance. He loves mentoring young people and believes in leaving your corner of the world a little better than you found it.

Tom and his wife, Beth, live in St. Joseph, Missouri, where they spend their free time traveling, collecting license plates and yo-yos, digging through antique stores, and cherishing time with their grandkids — who call them PaPa and BeBe. On weekends, you might also find Tom riding the rails at Worlds of Fun amusement park, working as part of the train crew.

Welts on Your Butt a Calf Could Suck is his first book — but not his last. He's already working on more collections of stories, as well as a heartfelt project about surviving a heart attack, and having faith, even when it hurts.

You Have to Leave If You Want to Come Back

Dad always had a way of slipping wisdom into the most inconvenient moments. We'd be packing up after a weekend with cousins, dragging our feet, begging for five more minutes—and he'd smile and say: "You have to leave if you want to come back."

At the time, it sounded like a grown-up trick. Now? It sounds like a book title.

This next batch of stories is filled with more tales from the gravel roads and back halls of memory—some funny, some thoughtful, a few that might make your eyes sting just a little. There are new adventures, untold confessions, second chances, and maybe even a sow with attitude.

Think of it as another lap around the old neighborhood. The mailbox might lean a little more. The road might be bumpier. But the stories are still there—waiting like porch lights left on.

So go ahead. Close this book. Stretch your legs. Get a snack.

Then come back.

We'll be right here—same spot, same voice, just a few more miles down the road.

Richardson & Company Press

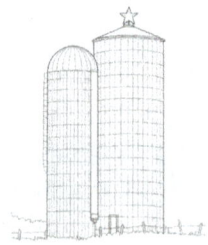

www.ingramcontent.com/pod-product-compliance
Lightning Source LLC
Chambersburg PA
CBHW061802120626
46550CB00005B/2102